BOOK
OF
GOMORRAH

BOOK OF GOMORRAH

An Eleventh-Century Treatise against Clerical Homosexual Practices

Peter Damian

Translated with an Introduction and Notes by
Pierre J. Payer

Wilfrid Laurier University Press

This book has been published with the help of a grant from the Humanities and Social Sciences Federation of Canada, using funds provided by the Social Sciences and Humanities Research Council of Canada. Wilfrid Laurier University Press acknowledges the financial support of the Government of Canada through the Canada Book Fund for its publishing activities.

Library and Archives Canada Cataloguing in Publication

Petro Damiani, Saint, 1007?–1072.
    [Liber Gomorrhianus. English]
    Book of Gomorrah

Includes bibliographical references and index.
ISBN 978-0-88920-123-1 (paper)
ISBN 978-0-88920-842-1 (e-book)

1. Homosexuality – Religious aspects – Catholic Church. 2. Catholic Church – Clergy – Sexual behavior. 3. Catholic Church – Doctrinal and controversial works. I. Payer, Pierre J., 1936– II. Title. III. Title: Liber Gomorrhianus. English.

BX1912.9.P3713   253′.2   C82-095146-3

CONTENTS

ACKNOWLEDGMENTS

Research for this translation was done in the course of a study of sexuality in the early Middle Ages which was undertaken with aid from the Social Sciences and Humanities Research Council and Mount Saint Vincent University. I would like to thank all those who read the work in its various stages and who made valuable comments. In particular I must acknowledge the helpful comments of the readers for the Canadian Federation for the Humanities and Dr. A. Monahan of St. Mary's University who checked the translation against the original Latin text. Needless to say errors and infelicities of translation are my own.

I am grateful to the University of Chicago Press for permission to use the translation of the letter of Pope Leo IX to Peter Damian which is contained in J. Boswell, *Christianity, Social Tolerance, and Homosexuality* (Chicago, 1980), pp. 365-66.

This book has been published with the help of a grant from the Canadian Federation for the Humanities, using funds provided by the Social Sciences and Humanities Research Council of Canada.

ABBREVIATIONS

Bailey, *Homosexuality* — D. S. Bailey, *Homosexuality and the Western Christian Tradition* (London, 1955).

Boswell, *Homosexuality* — J. Boswell, *Christianity, Social Tolerance, and Homosexuality: Gay People in Western Europe from the Beginning of the Christian Era to the Fourteenth Century* (Chicago, 1980).

Fliche, *La réforme* — A. Fliche, *La réforme grégorienne*. Vol. 1, *La formation des idées grégoriennes* (Paris, 1924).

Lucchesi, "Per una vita" — G. Lucchesi, "Per una vita di San Pier Damiani. Componenti cronologiche e topografiche," in *San Pier Damiano nel IX centenario della morte (1072-1972)* (Cesana, 1972, 1973), Vol. 1, 13-179; Vol. 2, 13-160.

MGH — *Monumenta Germaniae historica* (Hanover, 1893-1911).

PL — J. P. Migne (ed.), *Patrologia, Series Latina* (Paris, 1844ff.).

Ryan, *Damiani* — J. J. Ryan, *Saint Peter Damiani and his Canonical Sources: A Preliminary Study in the Antecedents of the Gregorian Reform* (Toronto, 1956).

INTRODUCTION

Homosexuality is a problem which North American society has not been successful in resolving. Polarized positions range from demonstrations in favour of "gay rights" and the legal protection of sexual preference to referenda for the repeal of overly liberal legislation and the barring of homosexual teachers from the schools. In often heated debates the anti-homosexual side is frequently characterized by deeply rooted religious attitudes fed by a tradition that is claimed to stretch back to the Old Testament. Throughout history opponents of homosexuality have brought against it the whole weight of divine law, natural law, ecclesiastical law, and criminal law. Today the churches too have entered the debate, particularly in reference to such questions as whether male homosexuals should be ordained to the ministry and whether practising homosexuals should be allowed full participation in the worship of the Christian community.

This contemporary social ferment and the simple imperatives of pastoral care have led many to examine the Christian tradition's approach to the question of homosexuality. These studies usually concentrate on four broad areas: (1) biblical teaching, (2) theological and legislative traditions, (3) modern psychological and sociological studies, (4) ethics and the pastoral ministry.[1] Although one sometimes detects a certain revisionist and exculpatory trend in the discussions of the first two areas, overall they are serious scholarly attempts to come to grips with what the ancient documents were really saying. A proper understanding of the Sodom and Gomorrah story, for instance, is

[1] See, e.g., "Episcopal Church to Launch Study on Homosexuality," *Canadian Churchman* 102/10 (1976); J. J. McNeil, *The Church and the Homosexual* (Kansas City, 1976); *Human Sexuality: New Directions in American Catholic Thought* (New York, 1977); *Homosexual People in Society*, by The Catholic Council for Church and Society (The Netherlands), trans. by B. A. Nachbahr (New Ways Ministry, 1980). For bibliographical material up to 1968 see M. Weinberg and A. Bell, *Homosexuality: An Annotated Bibliography* (New York, 1972).

important not so that it can be said that those who used it in the past to support censures of homosexuality were misguided but to assure that past uses not be repeated in the future. These exercises in biblical and historical scholarship are not luxuries which the heirs of the Christian tradition may or may not undertake. Christianity is a religion rooted in the Bible and tradition, not simply in the sense that it has a past but in the sense that it draws its food and nourishment through those roots. Its self-consciousness today and its hopes for tomorrow are fashioned out of a dialogue with the tradition, with what has been handed down over centuries. Frequently this tradition is felt as a heavy burden which inhibits efforts to move in directions which contemporary needs seem to demand.

This tradition regarding homosexuality is a classic example of a burden from the past which makes accommodation to these contemporary needs difficult for many. Nothing is to be gained by denying the past, however. What is needed is an understanding of the treatment of homosexuality, the reasons for its censures, a dossier of the biblical and ecclesiastical texts which were used to support the censures, and a more accurate interpretation of the sense and purpose of these texts in their own setting. It is only through such studies that the heirs of the Christian tradition will be able to move beyond their history, with self-conscious understanding of the past and a reasoned rejection of some facets of the tradition, toward a new synthesis in response to the demands and insights of today.

Unfortunately, historical studies of the early medieval treatment of homosexuality are not numerous, and, until the present, one has had to depend on the general work of Bailey, which covers the whole Western tradition, and a few other studies.[2] More recently, the work of John Boswell, which deals with the subject up to the fourteenth century, is a welcome contribution to this neglected area of study.[3]

---

[2] Bailey, *Homosexuality*. See V. L. Bullough, *Sexual Variance in Society and History* (New York, 1976), 363-64; A. Gauthier, "La sodomie dans le droit canonique médiévale," in B. Roy (ed.), *L'érotisme au moyen âge: Etudes presentées au Troisième colloque de l'Institut d'études médiévales* (Montreal, 1977), 109-22; M. Goodich, *The Unmentionable Vice: Homosexuality in the Later Medieval Period* (Santa Barbara, CA, 1979).

[3] Boswell, *Homosexuality*. Aside from the stated theme, the volume has chapters on Roman practices, the Scriptures, and Saint Paul's vocabulary, and an appendix containing translations of a number of texts relating to homosexuality.

In his book Bailey devotes a few pages to Peter Damian's *Liber Gomorrhianus (Book of Gomorrah)* which he calls "in some respects the most notable medieval pronouncement upon the subject of homosexual practices," and "this extraordinary composition."[4] In fact, the work is unique in the medieval Christian literature of the West since it is the only continuous prose treatment of the various forms of homosexuality, the circumstances of clerical offences, and the proposed measures against such behaviour. The later sermon-like section of the tract is revealing in the attitudes which its language betrays toward homosexual offences. Again, in Bailey's words it is "a treatise which has considerable interest as the record of an attitude to homosexual practices no less common at the present than in the past."[5] Although these remarks were written in 1955 in England, they are as applicable now to North American society as they were then for Britain.

As we shall see, the early Middle Ages abound in scattered references to homosexuality, usually in penitential and legislative contexts. The *Book of Gomorrah* stands out as a carefully planned and eloquently executed discussion of the subject reflecting both a legalistic concern with correct ecclesiastical censure and a passionate pastoral concern for those caught up in the behaviour. Damian's tract is a unique witness to historical attitudes and ideas about homosexuality. Even though its fierce anti-homosexual position would still find a responsive chord in many contemporaries, the value of the work today does not lie in providing such persons with support for their views. Rather, its value lies in the contribution it can make to understanding a characteristic Western approach to homosexuality. Social scientists, students of religion, and social historians who wish to acquire an insight into the traditional opposition to homosexuality will find the *Book of Gomorrah* an indispensable work both because it is the only extended, serious treatment of the subject in the formative period of the Christian West, and because it is such a clear expression of a tradition which is only hinted at in isolated pieces of legislation or in occasional theological questions.

As valuable as the work might be, however, it is a closed book for contemporary readers inasmuch as the majority of them do not read

Unfortunately the brief bibliography does not reflect the wealth of sources used in the book.

[4] Bailey, *Homosexuality*, 111.
[5] Ibid.

Latin. It is for this reason that an English translation of the *Book of Gomorrah* is offered here—to my knowledge, the first translation into any language.

Needless to say, Damian's work, like any document from a different time and place, requires more than casual attention on the part of the modern reader. The actual problematic, the rhetorical style, and the patterns of thought evidenced in the treatise are characteristic of a different age than our own. To this extent the work demands some concentration. On the other hand, the message and thrust of the arguments come through clearly and straightforwardly. There is no mistaking what Peter Damian has to say about what he saw as a serious problem and about how it was to be handled. This brief introduction will simply place Damian's work in the context of the early medieval treatment of homosexuality and attempt to resolve a few questions of interpretation. Wherever possible, reference will be made to relevant English works. The text of the introduction is meant to be intelligible on its own, with many of the notes serving a supplementary role for those who might wish to pursue the matter further.

Censures of Homosexuality Prior to 1048

The condemnation of homosexual practices is not an uncommon feature of the regulative literature of the early medieval church. The penitentials, which originated in Ireland in the latter half of the sixth century, frequently mention homosexual offences and provide for a wide range of penances. Most of the penitentials from the sixth century to the tenth century have at least one canon on homosexuality, but more often than not they have several canons censuring the various forms of homosexual behaviour which are outlined by Damian in his first chapter.[6] Two of the most important early collections of ecclesias-

[6] For an English introduction to the penitentials see J. McNeill and H. Gamer, *Medieval Handbooks of Penance: A Translation of the Principal* libri poenitentiales *and Selections from Related Documents* (Records of Civilization, Sources and Studies 29; New York, 1938); Bailey, *Homosexuality*, 100-10, discusses homosexuality in the penitentials. In addition to the materials translated in McNeill and Gamer the Irish penitentials are edited and translated in L. Bieler, *The Irish Penitentials*, with an appendix by D. A. Binchy (Scriptores Latini Hiberniae, Vol. 5; Dublin, 1963). The most recent introduction is that of C. Vogel, *Les "Libri Paenitentiales"* (Typologie des sources du moyen âge occidental 27; Turnhout,

tical canons, one at the beginning of the tenth century, the other a century later, incorporate a number of penitential canons on homosexuality.[7] One of these collectors, the eleventh-century bishop Burchard of Worms, in addition to material borrowed from previous works, also provides an original penitential which includes some startlingly vivid descriptions of various homosexual practices.[8]

On the other hand, prior to 1048 censures of such practices by ecclesiastical councils are rare. Aside from an early reference to pederasty in the Spanish Council of Elvira (ca. A.D. 306)[9] and canons 16 and 17 of the Council of Ancyra (ca. A.D. 314)[10] which became the standard source for medieval ecclesiastical legislation against homosexuality, there are only three conciliar references to this offence:

> Council of Toledo (A.D. 693), canon 3;[11]
> Council of Paris (A.D. 829), canon 34, canon 69;[12]
> Council of Trosly (A.D. 909), canon 15.[13]

However, there are several references to homosexuality in various documents of the Carolingian period:[14]

1978). For English translations of early penitential canons on homosexuality see Bieler, *Irish Penitentials*, 69 (Synod of the Grove of Victory), 75 (Penitential of Vinnian), 115 and 129 (Penitential of Cummean). See the Index in McNeill and Gamer, *Medieval Handbooks*, under "Homosexuality" and "Sodomy."

[7] See Regino of Prüm (A.D. 906) in H. Wasserschleben, *Reginonis abbatis Prumiensis: libri duo de synodalibus causis et disciplinis ecclesiasticis* (Leipzig, 1840), Book 2, chs. 249, 250, 251, 255, 370. Burchard of Worms (ca. A.D. 1008), *Decretum* 17.27, 28, 29, 34, 39 (PL 140, 924C-25C).

[8] See the edition of Burchard, *Decretum* 19.5 in H. J. Schmitz, *Die Bussbücher und das kanonische Bussverfahren nach handschriftlichen Quellen dargestellt* (Düsseldorf, 1898), nos. 120, 121, 122 (pp. 435-36), nos. 154, 155, 156 (p. 433, lesbian relations).

[9] Canon 71 (PL 84, 309B).

[10] PL 84, 107D. Bailey, *Homosexuality*, 86-89, discusses these canons; see also Boswell, *Homosexuality*, 178, n. 33.

[11] PL 84, 538A-D. This canon is partially translated by Bailey, *Homosexuality*, 93.

[12] See A. Werminghoff, *Concilia aevi Karolini*, Vol. 1/2, MGH, Legum sectio 3, Vol. 2, no. 50, pp. 634, 669.

[13] J. D. Mansi (ed.), *Sacrorum conciliorum nova et amplissima collectio* (Florence et al., 1758 ff.), Vol. 18A, 306.

[14] Bailey, *Homosexuality*, 94, no. 4, and 95, nos. 1, 3, 4, 5, appears to present documentary evidence for the Carolingian period, but his use of Mansi's edition of

1. *From the court of Charlemagne*:

General Admonition (A.D. 789), no. 49: reminder of the heavy penances of the Council of Ancyra for homosexuality and bestiality and ordering bishops and priests to root out the practice from among the people.[15]

Capitulary for Imperial Legates (*missi*), A.D. 802, no. 17: response to news of monastic abuses, one of which was homosexuality.[16]

2. *Collection of Benedictus Levita*:[17]

1, 82:   General Admonition (A.D. 789), no. 49.[18]

3, 143:   Homosexuality is listed among numerous offences which must be avoided. The kingdom is being torn apart because of them.[19]

3, 356:   Reference to bestiality, incest, and homosexuality, using the *Hispana* version of the council of Ancyra, canon 16. Those guilty of these crimes are to be punished with death, or, if allowed to live, are to do penance in accord with the council of Ancyra.[20]

3, 378:   From the Second Diocesan Statute of Theodulf of Orleans, ch. 14 (see below).[21]

Addition 2, 21 and Addition 4, 160: From the council of Paris (829), canon 69. Homosexuality is one of the evils for which the people are punished with famine and

---

the councils and capitularies results in considerable confusion, and aside from his mention of Isaac of Langres (94, no. 4) he omits reference to other diocesan statutes. Rather than attempt to sort out the confusion in Bailey, I offer a corrected list of the documentary evidence for references to homosexuality in the Carolingian period. See now Boswell, *Homosexuality*, 177-78.

[15] In A. Boretius, *Capitularia regum francorum*, MGH, Legum sectio 2, Vol. 1, no. 22. In the collection of Ansegisus 1, 48 (PL 97, 513D). Ansegisus compiled a collection of previous capitularies about A. D. 827. I have used the edition in PL 97, but there is a superior edition by A. Boretius, *Ansegisi abbatis capitularium collectio*, in *Capitularia regum francorum*, MGH, Legum sectio 2, Vol. 1, 382ff.

[16] In A. Boretius, *Capitularia regum francorum*, no. 33 (p. 95).

[17] One of the Pseudo-Isidorian forgeries from about A.D. 857, in PL 97, 699-912.

[18] PL 97, 712D.

[19] PL 97, 143A.

[20] PL 97, 842D.

[21] PL 97, 813A.

pestilence, the condition of the church is weakened, and the kingdom is endangered.[22]

3. *Diocesan Statutes*

From the beginning of the ninth century until well into the tenth a form of pastoral literature was popular which is usually referred to as diocesan statutes.[23] These were sets of regulations issued by bishops for the priests of their dioceses reminding them of ecclesiastical legislation, combatting contemporary abuses, and sometimes publicizing the acts of local synods. Censures of homosexual practices are also to be found in these documents:

> Second Diocesan Statute of Theodulf of Orleans, ch. 14: Admonishing priests to set an example by their own lives for the people to follow.
>
> Ibid., chs. 34-44: An extended treatment of homosexuality, bestiality, and incest.[24]
>
> Diocesan statute of MS Vat. Reg. lat. 612, ch. 8 (1): Because of homosexuality kingdoms are destroyed and delivered into the hands of the pagans. Every Christian should guard himself against this crime and those not polluted by it should beware lest they fall.[25]
>
> Rodulph of Bourges (ca. A.D. 850), *Capitula*, ch. 43: Repetition of Ancyra, canon 16.[26]

[22] PL 97, 866C, 909A; see Boswell, *Homosexuality*, 177, n. 30.

[23] For a study of the early diocesan statutes see J. Gaudemet, "Les statuts épiscopaux de première décade du IXe siècle," *Proceedings of the Fourth International Congress of Medieval Canon Law*, edited by S. Kuttner (Monumenta iuris canonici, Series C: Subsidia, 5; Vatican City, 1976), 303-49. See also P. Brommer, "Die bischöfliche Gesetzgebung Theodulfs von Orléans," *Zeitschrift der Savigny-Stiftung für Rechtsgeschichte*, Kanonistische Abteilung, 60 (1974), 32-37.

[24] Theodulf of Orleans, "Second Diocesan Statute," in C. De Clercq (ed.), *La législation religieuse franque de Clovis à Charlemagne: Etude sur les actes de conciles et les capitulaires, les statuts diocésains et les règles monastiques, 507-814* (Louvain, 1936), 327, 335-38. Also in PL 105, 211A, 214A-215C. De Clercq dates the statute to A.D. 787-818.

[25] In P. Finsterwalder, "Zwei Bischofskapitularien der Karolingerzeit," *Zeitschrift der Savigny-Stiftung für Rechtsgeschichte*, Kanonistische Abteilung, 14 (1925), 359.

[26] PL 119, 723D (= Council of Ancyra, canon 16) in an early Latin collection of councils and papal letters called the Dionysio-Hadriana (PL 67, 154C).

> Herard of Tours (858), *Capitula*, ch. 11: "Those who sin irration-
> ally [allusion to Ancyra, canon 16], or with relatives are to
> be severely judged so that such vices might be cut away."[27]

References to homosexuality are not numerous in the regulative
literature of the Carolingian era when compared to the vast body of
regulations enacted after 789 by political and ecclesiastical bodies. The
texts cited above invite the judgment that, while not unheard of,
homosexuality was certainly not perceived to be a particularly pressing
problem. However, they do not warrant the remark that the legislation
"amounts to nothing more than the routine repetition of existing
laws."[28]

The passing reference to pollution "with men or animals" by the
Council of Trosly (A.D. 909) is the only conciliar statement on the
question in the tenth century, but Hefele's remark should be borne in
mind; "The tenth century, so poor in synodal assemblies, stands in
sharp contrast to the ninth in the course of which we encountered such
a great number."[29]

Before leaving this topic mention should be made of another facet of
medieval literary history. From the time of Regino of Prüm
(A.D. 906) up to 1048 and long afterwards numerous works in canon
law were compiled consisting largely of excerpts from ecclesiastical
councils, papal letters, the writings of the Fathers of the church, and
the penitentials.[30] These canonical collections were designed to pass on
the tradition of ecclesiastical legislation and were often meant for
practical pastoral reference. It would be cumbersome and of little value
in an introduction of this sort to itemize references, but I might
indicate that after a careful study of numerous collections up to 1048,
both printed and in manuscript, I found that every one contains a
number of texts censuring homosexual practices. Taken together with
the tradition of the penitentials it is clear that prior to 1048 the church
displayed a consistent and uninterrupted pastoral concern with homosexuality. It must be remembered that the absence of new official
legislation is not necessarily a measure of concern with behaviour

[27] PL 121, 765A.

[28] Bailey, *Homosexuality*, 95.

[29] K. J. Hefele and H. Leclercq, *Histoire des conciles* (Paris, 1911), Vol. 4, 721
(my translation).

[30] See P. Fournier and G. Le Bras, *Histoire des collections canoniques en occident
depuis les Fausses Décrétales jusqu'au Décret de Gratien*, Vol. 1 (Paris, 1931).

believed to be immoral. As the forum for dealing with these offences was private penance, it is in materials designed to aid the confessor that one should look for directions regarding the treatment of homosexuality. Both the penitentials and the sections dealing with sins and confession in the collections of canon law provide overwhelming evidence that homosexuality was included in the catalogues of sins worthy of frequent mention. On the other hand, it is true that it was "rarely singled out for special hostility" at this time.[31]

Early Reform Movements

It is generally recognized that in the course of the tenth century and the first half of the eleventh the moral life of the church deteriorated in continental Europe and at Rome in particular. Simony and clerical sexual immorality were felt to be the two central problems.[32] Powerful lay control and ecclesiastical weakness frequently led to the purchase of high ecclesiastical office for money or for other considerations, and an enfeebled papal authority in Rome showed little inclination to correct the abuse. At the same time the rules against clerical marriage seemed everywhere to be disregarded.

It is true that at the same time as these abuses were weakening the church frequent attempts at reform were undertaken. From its founding in A.D. 910 the Cluniac order represented a strong, independent stand particularly against the declining monastic life, but its ideals were not those for a secular, political society.[33] Occasionally particular bishops attempted to reform the situation in their own dioceses, and from the beginning of the eleventh century even the German emperors showed an interest in initiating reforms but without relinquishing political hegemony over ecclesiastical affairs.[34] As Fliche points out, all of these attempts were bound to fail without a strong, independent papacy to foster and promote them.[35] It is for this reason that he dates the beginning of the pre-Gregorian reform to the election to the papacy of Bruno of Toul who took the name of Leo IX (A.D. 1048-1054).[36]

---

[31] *Human Sexuality* (cited above, n. 1), 197.
[32] See Fliche, *La réforme*, 1-38.
[33] See H. E. J. Cowdrey, *The Cluniacs and the Gregorian Reform* (Oxford, 1970).
[34] See Fliche, *La réforme*, 39-113.
[35] Ibid., 113.
[36] Ibid., 128; for Leo IX and the reforms of the period see ibid., 129-59;

Peter Damian

At the time of Leo's accession to the papacy in Rome, Peter Damian was busy working for the reform of monastic institutions and clerical morals from his base at the monastery of Fonte Avellana in the diocese of Gubbio in central Italy. Born in 1007, Damian was to become a leading figure as monk, cleric, bishop, and cardinal who played an active role both in encouraging general ecclesiastical reform and in working strenuously to promote it.[37] His reforming activities took him throughout Italy and into France and Germany, placing him in an ideal position to be familiar with the state of the church in his day. But above all he was a monk who opted for a life of contemplation, prayer, and mortification, finally successful in resigning his high ecclesiastical office (A.D. 1069) and returning to the monastic life he loved so much.

In addition to his activities in support of reform Peter Damian left a legacy of writings which themselves assure him a singular place in the history of Christian spirituality. He addressed himself to all levels of secular and ecclesiastical society, encouraging his recipients to the ideals of Christian living.[38] Some might find his writings harsh in places, but it must be remembered that he was writing in a harsh age which in many quarters had lost sight of the goal of Christian spirituality. One of his consistent themes was an attack on the sexual immorality of the clergy and the laxness of superiors who refused to take a strong hand against it.

W. Ullmann, *A Short History of the Papacy in the Middle Ages* (London: University Paperback, 1974), 128-41.

[37] The finest general introduction to Damian is J. Leclercq, *Saint Pierre Damien ermite et homme d'Eglise* (Uomini et dottrine, 8; Rome, 1960). See Fliche, *La réforme*, 175-264; J. Whitney, "Peter Damiani and Humbert," *The Cambridge Historical Journal* 1 (1925), 225-48; O. J. Blum, "The Monitor of the Popes: St. Peter Damian," *Studi Gregoriani* 2 (1947), 459-76; and K. Little, "The Personal Development of Peter Damian," in *Order and Innovation: Essays in Honor of Joseph R. Strayer* (Princeton, 1976), 317-41.

[38] See O. J. Blum, *St. Peter Damian: His Teaching on the Spiritual Life* (Washington, DC, 1947); J. Leclercq, F. Vandenbroucke, and L. Bouyer, *The Spirituality of the Middle Ages*, trans. by The Benedictines of Holme Eden Abbey (New York, 1968), 97-100.

Book of Gomorrah

Peter perhaps sensed the possibilities for reform in Pope Leo IX since it is to him that he addressed his *Book of Gomorrah*, the first of his works censuring clerical sexual abuses.[39] The fact that the work was sent to Leo dates it to 1048-1054, the period of Leo's papacy, but there is little to narrow the date further. Leo's reply to Damian, which is prefaced to the edition of Damian's work in the Migne edition of his works, is listed by Jaffé as being of uncertain date.[40] Even if Peter Damian's letter 1.4 was written in regard to the *Book of Gomorrah* there is nothing in that letter to date it precisely. The most commonly accepted date seems to be 1049 and some would place the *Book of Gomorrah* after the Council of Reims (fall of 1049) but I have been unable to find any rationale for this exact dating.

Whatever the date, the work was like an opening volley in Damian's continued fight against clerical sexual behaviour and the first in a long line of tracts and countertracts on the subject which would characterize the reform movement until the end of the century.[41] In the words of Dom Leclercq, the *Book of Gomorrah* is precise and clear, tactfully introducing the required nuances without being vulgar or obscene.[42]

Although the tract is addressed to Leo IX, the structure of the work suggests that it was also meant to be read by those clerics who were actually engaged in homosexual practices. There is a canonical section (Preface, chs. 1-16, 26), which is addressed to the Pope, and a pastoral section (chs. 17-25), addressed to the offenders.[43] The main purpose of

[39] The following are Damian's more important works on clerical sexual abuses. The dates are those provided in the updated recent work of G. Lucchesi, "Per una vita," Vol. 1, Appendix 6, "Datazione piu' probabile di lettere e di opusculi di S. Pier Damiani," pp. 148-60. Opusc. 17 (PL 145, 379-88), written in A.D. 1059; Letter 1.15 to Pope Alexander II (PL 144, 225-35), written in A. D. 1063; Opusc, 18.2 (PL 145, 398-416), written in A.D. 1064; Opusc, 18.3 (PL 145, 416-24), written in A.D. 1064; Opusc. 47 (PL 145, 709-16), written in A.D. 1065; Opusc. 18.1 (PL 145, 387-98), written between A.D. 1069 and 1072.

[40] PL 145, 159-60; see *Regesta pontificum romanorum* (to A.D. 1143), edited by P. Jaffé, 2nd. ed. by G. Wattenbach, S. Loewenfeld, F. Kaltenbrunner, and P. Ewald (Leipzig, 1885), no. 4311 (3275), dated, A.D. 1049-54. See the appendix for a translation of Leo's letter.

[41] For a summary of these tracts see C. Mirbt, *Die Publizistik im Zeitalter Gregors VII*, "Der Kampf um den Priestercölibat" (Leipzig, 1894), 239-342.

[42] Leclercq, *Saint Pierre Damien*, 70.

[43] By "canonical section" I mean that part of the work in which Damian

the *Book of Gomorrah* is clear. Peter Damian, who was in doubt whether clerical offenders should be punished with deposition from their ecclesiastical rank for engaging in homosexual behaviour, wrote to the Pope requesting answers to several specific questions (ch. 26).

Concerns of the *Book of Gomorrah*

What is not clear is the precise nature of some of the problems that alarmed Damian. In the first chapter he outlines three forms of homosexual activity (in addition to masturbation which he seems to put in the same class of acts against nature), but he is not always clear as to the agents and circumstances of the activities. He is alarmed by the spread of homosexual behaviour among the clergy (Preface) but does not specify whether he means secular clergy, monastic clergy, or both. We know he has priests in mind since the two circumstances he does describe both involve confessors.

In the one case he condemns priests who, after engaging in homosexual acts together, confess to one another (ch. 7); in the other, he censures confessors who engage in such behaviour with their male penitents (ch. 9). He also attacks the lower clergy in an impassioned argument against those "sodomists" who attempt to break into sacred orders (ch. 5). There is an ambiguous phrase in Damian which mentions falling "with eight or even ten other equally sordid men" (ch. 2). It is not clear whether this is a reference to promiscuous sequential acts with several different men. Pope Leo's reply, which uses the phrase "with several," is equally vague. I assume that these references are not to group activity since I have never encountered a reference to such practices in any other treatment of sexual behaviour in the early medieval period.

Damian's reference to "spiritual sons" in chapter eight is a reference to the male penitents with whom confessors were having sexual relations. This seems to be the first use of this expression and signals a concern which I do not believe has precedent in the penitential and canonical literature. There were previous references to spiritual daughters but these censures applied to sexual relations with godchil-

provides arguments for the deposition of homosexual clerics and in which he argues against the penitential penances in favour of what he considers more authentic ecclesiastical censures.

dren or with those whom a priest had baptized.[44] An echo, somewhat after Damian's time, of this concern about having sexual relations with penitents is to be found in Bonizo of Sutri's *Book of the Christian Life* which introduces a canon entitled, "Who are the spiritual sons of priests?"[45] The following canon censures the priest who "for reasons of fornication approaches his [female] penitent."[46]

The two specific abuses, then, which Peter Damian singles out for particular mention are priests who confess to each other after sinning together, and priests who sin with their male penitents. He also wants to bar homosexual offenders from becoming priests.[47]

Damian's Arguments

The canonical section of the *Book of Gomorrah* deals directly with the problem of homosexuality, the arguments in favour of deposition of offending priests, and in the last chapter requests the Pope to appoint a commission to study the problem and to reply to Damian's questions so that his doubts and the doubts of others might be resolved.[48] In support of his claim for the deposition of priests guilty of homosexual behaviour Damian argues both positively and negatively. The negative argument consists in a perceptive attack on the value and authority of the conflicting and inconsistent canons found in the penitentials, what he calls the apocryphal canons (chs. 10-12). He sets these inauthentic sources against the authentic tradition represented by the Council of Ancyra (chs. 13-14), St. Basil (ch. 15; actually Fructuosus), and Pope Siricius (ch. 15). This method of resolving contradictory authorities

---

[44] See the Penitential of Monte Cassino, canon 25 in J. Schmitz, *Die Bussbücher und die Bussdisciplin der Kirche nach handschriftlichen Quellen dargestellt* (Mainz, 1883), 406; the *Collection in Nine Books* in Vatican Library, MS 1349, Book 9.40, 42 (fols. 203rb, 203vb).

[45] Book 10.44 in E. Perels (ed.), *Bonizo: Liber de vita christiana* (Berlin, 1930), 331.

[46] Ibid., 321. See the discussion in Peter Damian, Opusc. 17 (PL 145, 384-85).

[47] Chapter 4 deals with an objection which Damian may have encountered. His point is that the presence of necessity and the absence of morally qualified priests is not an excuse for morally unqualified priests to meet the necessity. This is one of the doubts he asks the Pope to resolve in chapter 26.

[48] Lucchesi, "Per una vita," Vol. 1, 83, suggests that Damian is requesting that the matter be presented for consideration by a synod.

anticipates Abelard's *Sic et Non* and Gratian's *Concordance of Discordant Canons* by almost a century.[49]

Damian's positive arguments generally share a common structure which might be called *a fortiori* arguments by analogy. That is, he introduces a text which actually deals with a subject other than the deposition of homosexual clerics, points out the sanction for that subject, and concludes that it should apply even more to priests who engage in homosexual practices. However, in no instance does he cite an ecclesiastical authority which sanctions deposition of clerics found guilty of homosexual actions.

The text from Gregory the Great (ch. 3) establishes that those who are guilty of an offence punishable by death in the Old Law cannot be ordained. It does not, however, establish that those already ordained should be deposed, which the title of the chapter suggests.　In the eighth chapter Damian attempts to argue from analogy that if clerics who have sexual relations with virgins are to be deposed then clerics who have sexual relations with their spiritual sons should also be deposed. This is a promising argument but it is only convincing if Damian establishes that deposition is the appropriate penalty for clerical intercourse with virgins. However, he fails to support this claim on any authoritative source, contenting himself with a rhetorical appeal to the common practice.

The use of the Council of Ancyra (chs. 13-14) indicates a faithful use of an accepted authority which had been the common legacy of ecclesiastical legislation for centuries. The principal value of this authority is again to provide a basis for an argument from analogy: If the church punished lay homosexual offenders with such severity, how much more ought clerical offenders to be penalized? It is interesting to note, however, that Damian passes over in silence the express provision of the sixteenth canon of Ancyra for the possibility of extending mercy to penitents whose quality of life warrants it.

To be sure, authorities on which Peter Damian could have based a convincing argument for deposition are not numerous. However, he did have available the canon of the Council of Toledo (A.D. 693)

---

[49] For a translation of the Prologue to the *Sic et Non* (A.D. 1122) in which Abelard discusses the problem of conflicting authorities see B. Polka and B. Zelechow (eds.), *Readings in Western Civilization* 1, *The Intellectual Adventure of Man to 1600* (Toronto, 1970), 102-14. Gratian (d. ca. A.D. 1159) was the first systematizer of ecclesiastical law.

referred to above, which provided for the deposition of priests engaged in homosexual practices. The very section in Burchard's *Decretum* from which Damian excerpted the penitential canons (ch. 10) begins with a text from the Canons of the Apostles which provides for the deposition of bishops, priests, and deacons caught in fornication, perjury, or theft. He could have argued for deposition from that text more plausibly than from the texts he used.

There is a curious omission from Damian's argument which must be explained either on the basis of conscious omission or ignorance. At least from the time of Rabanus Maurus in the ninth century there were in circulation several dossiers of texts dealing with the problem of whether "fallen" (*lapsi*) priests should be deposed.[50] This is not the place to examine each in detail but a reading of these dossiers will show that the problem was not posed in the simple terms of deposition or no deposition, but rather with respect to whether the offence was publicly known or done and confessed in secret. In the former case deposition was to be the rule because of the attendant scandal; in the latter case the priest was to do genuine penance and then could recoup his position. It is difficult to imagine that Peter Damian even in 1049 would not have been familiar with some form of this dossier. It can be taken as certain that he was familiar with the texts in Burchard's *Decretum* 19.42 and 43 since, as we shall see, he uses excerpts from St. John Chrysostom taken from *Decretum* 19.44-48. I suspect the texts of Burchard were passed over because they contradicted Damian's position on the wholesale

---

[50] See Rabanus Maurus, *Paenitentiale ad Otgarium*, ch. 1, "Of those who commit capital crimes after sacred ordination and of their penance or excommunication" (PL 112, 1399), and the same subject by the same author in *Paenitentiale ad Heribaldum*, ch. 10 (PL 110, 474D). See R. Kottje, *Die Bussbücher Halitgars von Cambrai und des Hrabanus Maurus* (Berlin and New York, 1980), 216-40, for discussion of the origin of this dossier. Hincmar of Reims, *Capitula*, "Those who confess or who are convicted of a crime are rightly to be deposed from their ecclesiastical rank" (PL 125, 786). Burchard, *Decretum* 19.42, "Of the lapsed, how they are to be corrected and consoled with fraternal love so that they do not fall into the snares of the devil and despair" (PL 140, 988B), and 19.43, "Whether the lapsed in sacred orders can be restored" (PL 140, 988D). In the *Collection in Two Books*, placed in the time of Leo IX by its recent editor, there are numerous texts on the question of deposition; see J. Bernhard, "La Collection en deux livres (Cod. Vat. lat. 3832)," *Revue de droit canonique* 12 (1962), Book 1, cc. 350-61. For criticism of Bernhard's dating see J. T. Gilchrist (ed.), *Diversorum patrum sententiae sive Collectio in LXXIV titulos digesta* (Monumenta iuris canonici, series B: Corpus collectionum 1; Vatican, 1973), xxi.

deposition of fallen priests. Damian himself has two dossiers of authorities on clerical celibacy, but none of the texts he uses is directly concerned with the question of deposition.[51] His own position, however, is stated clearly in another work: "Those who are not ashamed of befouling the purity of ecclesiastical chastity should be deposed."[52]

It would appear that on the question of deposition Damian was attempting to make law, not to reflect tradition. Many of the texts collected by Rabanus Maurus, Hincmar of Reims, Burchard of Worms, and the *Collection in Two Books* leave open the possibility of a priest's reinstatement in certain circumstances after a serious offence. Peter Damian's *Book of Gomorrah* argues against this tradition in its appeal for the indiscriminate deposition of clerics who had engaged in homosexual acts.

In his reply Pope Leo not only differs from Damian but seems to issue a mild rebuke.[53] In an apparent attempt to pacify him the Pope agrees that in his own judgment and in the judgment of the sacred canons those who sin in the four ways outlined by Damian should be deposed. However, he goes on immediately to say that he is going to act "more humanely" (*humanius*), distinguishing between circumstances which merit deposition and others which do not. It is the use of "more humanely" that appears to be a rebuke. Damian had, in his text, already berated certain rectors of churches for being "more humane" (*humaniores*) than was expedient (ch. 2) while here we have the supreme rector of the church claiming to act "more humanely."

Leo neither responds directly to Damian's questions nor does he draw on the distinction between public and private offences. Rather, he distinguishes among various modalities of the acts themselves. The Pope wills and orders that if the following were not long-term or promiscuous offenders, if they curbed their desires, and did approved penance they were to be readmitted to their former ecclesiastical rank: those committing solitary masturbation; those committing mutual masturbation; those committing femoral fornication. The following should give up hope of being readmitted: those committing solitary masturbation over a long time, or mutual masturbation promiscuously even for a short time; those committing anal fornication (sodomy).

---

[51] See Opusc. 18.2 (PL 145, 400) and Letter 5.13 (PL 144, 358).
[52] Opusc. 17 (PL 145, 386B).
[53] Leo's letter is translated in the appendix.

Although this reply did not directly respond to each of Peter's questions, it provided principles for answering them. Finally, the Pope warns that, "If anyone shall dare to criticize or question this decree of apostolic direction, let him know that he is himself acting in peril of his rank."

Pastoral Concern

It was suggested above that the *Book of Gomorrah* was meant to be read by the offenders themselves. This is evident from what was called the pastoral section of the work (chs. 17-25) and seems to be anticipated by Damian in chapter 25 where he attempts to defend himself against possible criticism. The pastoral section is a series of impassioned pleas which are addressed to the "carnal man," "unhappy soul," "miserable soul," "condemned carnal men"—descriptions which hardly fit the Pope. It is true that in another work addressed to Pope Nicholas II on clerical celibacy Damian's direct address to the sinner is a literary device. He says, "But since I would not dare to insult even slightly the supreme bishop of the universal church, I will briefly address the sinner."[54] There then follows a chapter entitled, "Against the Priest Given over to Lust." However, the nine chapters in the *Book of Gomorrah* which are addressed to the sinner are more than a literary ruse. They are the heart-felt outpouring of a man who is genuinely interested in moving souls to repentance and hope. They would have no place in this work if they were not meant to reach those clerics who were engaged in homosexual practices.

Most of the material in the pastoral section is Damian's own original composition woven around a texture of biblical citations. However, there are a few phrases in chapter 17 and several in chapter 23 which seem to be taken from Burchard, *Decretum* 19.44, 46, 48, which are excerpts from the famous work of John Chrysostom to the priest Theodore after his fall.[55]

---

[54] Opüsc. 17 (PL 145, 384B).

[55] Greek text with French translation in *Jean Chrysostome à Theodore*, edited and translated by J. Dumortier (Sources chrétiennes 117; Paris, 1966); English translation by W. R. Stephens, *An Exhortation to Theodore after His Fall* (Nicene and Post-Nicene Fathers, 1st series, Vol. 9; New York, 1889), 91-111; 111-16. The Latin parallels are as follows:

Was Homosexuality a Problem?

A word must be said about a question that invariably occurs to a reader of the *Book of Gomorrah*: Did actual circumstances prompt Peter Damian to write this work? Bailey says that it is uncertain whether the tract has any historical value in providing evidence for the extent of homosexual practices in Damian's day.[56] He seems to be unwilling to take at face value Damian's assertion that, "A certain abominable and terribly shameful vice has grown up in our region" (Preface). The expression "in our region" (*in nostris partibus*) is used frequently by Damian in contexts in which he is speaking about local conditions. Lucchesi chronicles at some length the interest Damian showed in the affairs of the region stretching far beyond his monastery at Fonte Avellana.[57]

Unfortunately, there is no corroborating evidence to support Damian's claim about homosexual problems in his area.[58] There is the

	Burchard, *Decretum* (PL 140)	*Book of Gomorrah* (PL 145)
19.44	"Quis dabit capiti . . . ." (991D-992A)	177B-177C
	"Si enim tantum . . . ." (992B)	184D-185A
	"Non enim peccatorum . . . ." (992B)	184D
	"Exsurge, exsurge . . . ." (993A)	184C
19.46	"Cecidit asinus . . . ." (994A)	185A
19.48	"Qualiter rogo . . . ." (994C)	185B

[56] Bailey, *Homosexuality*, 111.

[57] See Lucchesi, "Per una vita," Vol. 1, 43-62, in the section entitled, "Pier Damiani e le diocesi 'in nostris partibus.'"

[58] There is a letter (1.4; PL 144, 208B) addressed by Damian to Pope Leo in which he defends himself against calumniating attacks which were circulating and which apparently had reached the Pope. Lucchesi, "Per una vita," Vol. 1, 83-84, takes the letter to be a defence against those who were protesting the *Book of Gomorrah*, which would indicate that Damian had perhaps touched a sore spot. In another letter (2.6; PL 144, 170A) written to Cardinals Hildebrand and Stephen (A.D. 1069), Damian complains that Pope Alexander II had taken a book from him and would not return it. Although it has been suggested that the work was the *Book of Gomorrah*, contemporary opinion is against this view; see Ryan, *Damiani*,

report of the Council of Reims (A.D. 1049) which records that homosexuality (*de sodomitico vitio*) was one of the subjects to be treated by the council, which apparently passed a canon against it.[59] It is impossible to know, however, whether the canon was issued because of a local problem of homosexuality in the area or because it was one of the offences of which Hughes of Langres was accused.[60]

Commentators generally take Damian's remarks at face value. Speaking about the more general problem of Rome in the first part of the eleventh century, Hefele says that rather than follow the lead of Cluny, Rome "plunged itself into simony and the corruption of the sodomist clergy."[61] Whitney says that Damian "came to deal with the worst kinds of sins, unhappily most prevalent then and there."[62] Fliche refers to sodomy "which was the rage particularly among the monks."[63] Mazzotti says that in the *Book of Gomorrah* Damian provides an analysis "of the abominable faults which were committed by many ecclesiastics."[64] Dressler says that the work proposes a "dismal picture of the moral state of the clergy of the day."[65]

155; Lucchesi, "Per una vita," Vol. 1, 109-10. Boswell, *Homosexuality*, 213, assumes that the work was the *Book of Gomorrah* but his arguments are not convincing. The letter was written twenty (not fifteen) years later and simply does not betray the title of the work in question. Boswell says (p. 213, n. 17) that at the time Damian was still trying to interest the papacy in the matter of homosexuality. He may very well have, but there is no indication in his writings after the *Book of Gomorrah* that Peter Damian ever returned to the subject.

[59] Anselm, *Historia dedicationis ecclesiae s. Remigii apud Remos* (PL 142, 1431C, 1437B). Anselm does not quote a canon against homosexuality but reports, "Likewise it also condemned sodomists" (1437B). For a discussion of this report, which was written down some years after the council, see Hefele and Leclercq, *Histoire des conciles* (cited above, n. 29), Vol. 4, 1011-28; Fliche, *La réforme*, Vol. 1, 136-45; S. Giet, "Le concile de Reims de 1049," *Mémoires de la société d'agriculture, commerce, sciences et arts du département de la Marne* 75 (1960), 31-36.

[60] Hughes, Bishop of Langres, was accused of numerous offences: buying his bishopric, selling sacred orders, murder, adultery, tyrannical rule over his clerics, sodomy, extortion by torture applied to the genitals. He admitted to having sold orders and extortion, but without torture; see PL 142, 1434A-35A.

[61] Hefele and Leclercq, *Histoire des conciles*, Vol. 4, 981 (my translation).

[62] J. P. Whitney, *Hildebrandine Essays* (Cambridge, 1932), 102.

[63] Fliche, *La réforme*, 191 (my translation).

[64] C. Mazzotti, "Il celibato e la castità del clero in S. Pier Damiano," in *Studi su S. Pier Damiano in onore de Cardinale Amleto Giovanni Cicognani* (Biblioteca cardinale Caetano Cicognani, 5; 2d ed.; Faenza, 1970), 347 (my translation).

[65] F. Dressler, *Petrus Damiani: Leben und Werk* (Studia Anselmiana 34; Rome, 1954), 100 (my translation). See Ryan, *Damiani*, 155, n. 107.

Certainly the reality of events is not verified on the basis of historians' statements. However, their interpretation often is, and the question here is the trustworthiness of Damian's statement that homosexuality had grown up among the clergy of his region. The scholars just cited have been adduced simply to indicate the absence of any serious caveat among respectable historians in taking Damian's claim at its face value. Given the general decline of sexual morality among the clergy at the time, the specific situations dealt with by Damian, and the fact that the Pope saw fit to respond to the *Book of Gomorrah*, it would seem reasonable to accept Damian's assertion. The specific situations dealt with by Peter Damian tell against Kühn's view that Damian had overgeneralized from a few individual cases, a view further developed by Bailey.[66]

Conclusion

To the extent that Peter Damian received a reply from the Pope to his questions in regard to the ecclesiastical censure of clerics engaged in homosexual practices, the *Book of Gomorrah* could be said to have been a success. However, it did not succeed in convincing the Pope to follow through on Damian's call for the indiscriminate deposition of such clerics. Whether or not the work succeeded in reversing the spread of homosexual practices in the areas which were of concern to Damian is unknown. All that can be said is that he never returned to an extended discussion of the theme again. I know of no use of the work by subsequent authors, but an excerpt from Leo's reply is contained in a later collection of canon law.[67]

The Translation

The challenge for a translator is to be faithful to the original while being as idiomatic as possible in the translation. I will not resurrect the

[66] See L. Kühn, *Petrus Damiani und seine Anschauungen über Staat und Kirche* (Karlsruhe, 1913), 3; Bailey, *Homosexuality*, 115: "His onslaught was probably provoked less by an outbreak of vice than by his revulsion from the conduct of a few licentious individuals which had come to his notice, and which served to sharpen the edge of his indignation."

[67] The *Polycarpus*, Paris, Bibl. nat. lat. 3881, fol. 134r, quotes an excerpt from Leo's reply to Damian.

ancient debate over whether a good translation should be one that translates word for word or idea for idea. In translating Peter Damian one must contend with the words, the ideas, and the rhythmic style which characterize his elegant writing. An introduction such as this, which is intended primarily for those who do not read Latin, is not the place to discuss problems of Latin translation. However, there is one point which should be made about an aspect of Damian's language which challenges English idiom. He frequently strings together words which seem to be used more for their emotive effect than for their cognitive value. One does not often encounter expressions such as "in the pigsty of filthy obscenity" or "who is polluted with a male by the filthy stain of sexual impurity." Such expressions, and they are frequent, perhaps do not sound quite right in English but there is no way of avoiding them short of departing from Damian's words altogether. It is hoped that the quaintness of the expressions does not detract from their real purpose, which is to arouse feelings, not to inform minds.

I have translated the text of the Gaetani edition of the *Liber Gomorrhianus* which is found in Migne, *Opusculum* 7 (PL 145, 161-90). It was my original intention to compare this edition with the earliest manuscript (Monte Cassino 358, pp. 131-50) containing the work but I was unsuccessful in my attempt to obtain a microfilm.[68]

As far as possible biblical quotations will follow the translation of *The New American Bible* (Boston, 1976) and the biblical books are abbreviated according to that edition. Frequently Damian's biblical citations do not correspond to the Vulgate text of the Bible.

Reference is made in the notes to untranslated Latin works. It was felt that this would enhance the value of the work for readers of Latin without taking away from the translation. However, wherever English translations do exist they will always be cited.

[68] The manuscripts of the works of Peter Damian are discussed by K. Reindel, "Studien zur Überlieferung der Werke des Petrus Damiani," *Deutsches Archiv* 15 (1959), 23-102; 16 (1960), 73-154; 18 (1962), 317-417.

BOOK OF GOMORRAH

PREFACE

Peter, the lowliest servant of monks, to the most Blessed Pope Leo, the homage of due respect:

Since it is known from the very mouth of Truth that the Apostolic See is the mother of all the churches, it is proper that, should a doubt arise from any source whatever which seems to pertain to the care of souls, we have recourse to her as to the teacher and font of heavenly wisdom. Then from this one head of ecclesiastical discipline a light will shine to dissipate the darkness of doubt and to illumine the whole body of the Church with the glittering brightness of truth.

A certain abominable and terribly shameful vice has grown up in our region. Unless the hand of severe punishment resists as soon as possible, there is certainly a danger that the sword of divine anger will be used savagely against it to the ruin of many. Alas! it is shameful to speak of, shameful to suggest such foul disgrace to sacred ears! But if the doctor shrinks in horror from infected wounds, who will take the trouble to apply the cauter? If the one who is to heal becomes nauseated, who will lead sick hearts back to health? Vice against nature creeps in like a cancer and even touches the order of consecrated men.[1] Sometimes it rages like a bloodthirsty beast in the midst of the sheepfold of Christ with such bold freedom that it would have been much healthier for many to have been oppressed under the yoke of a secular army than to be freely delivered over to the iron rule of diabolical tyranny under the cover of religion, particularly when this is

---

[1] For the image of a spreading cancer, see Peter Damian, Letter 1.13 (PL 144, 219B); Opusc. 8 (PL 145, 203D); Opusc. 17 (PL 145, 386B).

accompanied by scandal to others. For Truth says, "Whoever scandalizes one of these little ones, it were better for him to have a great millstone hung around his neck and to be drowned in the depths of the sea."[2]

Unless the strength of the Apostolic See intervenes as soon as possible, there is no doubt but that this unbridled wickedness, even though it should wish to be restrained, will be unable to stop on its headlong course.

[2] Matt. 18:6.

I

THE DIFFERENT TYPES OF THOSE WHO
SIN AGAINST NATURE

Four types of this form of criminal wickedness can be distinguished
in an effort to show you the totality of the whole matter in an orderly
way: some sin with themselves alone; some commit mutual masturbation; some commit femoral fornication; and finally, others commit the
complete act against nature.[3] The ascending gradation among these is
such that the last mentioned are judged to be more serious than the
preceding. Indeed, a greater penance is imposed on those who fall with
others than on those who defile only themselves; and those who
complete the act are to be judged more severely than those who are
defiled through femoral fornication. The devil's artful fraud devises
these degrees of falling into ruin such that the higher the level the
unfortunate soul reaches in them, the deeper it sinks in the depths of
hell's pit.

[3] Ryan, *Damiani* (28, text 15) suggests that this division is a summary of the
detailed descriptions in Burchard's "Interrogatory for Confessors," *Decretum* 19.5
(PL 140, 967D-68B). The expressions "mutual masturbation" and "femoral fornication" are used to render what are literally "some by the hands of others" and
"others between the thighs" respectively. See the very old (ca. A.D. 550) division
in the Synod of the Grove of Victory, canon 8 in Bieler, *Irish Penitentials*, 69. For
some reason Bieler does not translate the details of this canon, which reads,
"Whoever commits the male crime as the Sodomites [shall do penance] for four
years; whoever in the thighs, three years; whoever by the hand of another or his
own, two years."

II

EXCESSIVE PIETY ON THE PART OF SUPERIORS FAILS TO EXCLUDE FROM ORDERS THOSE WHO FALL IN THIS WAY

It is true that those liable to this ruin frequently come to their senses through the generosity of divine mercy, make satisfaction, and even piously receive the burden of penance no matter how heavy; but they are utterly terrified of losing their ecclesiastical status.[4] And some rectors of churches who are perhaps more humane in regard to this vice than is expedient absolutely decree that no one ought to be deposed from his order on account of three of the grades which were enumerated above. They maintain that only those should be degraded who have clearly fallen into the ultimate act. Consequently, when someone is known to have fallen into this wickedness with eight or even ten other equally sordid men, we see him still remaining in his ecclesiastical position.

Surely this impious piety does not cut off the wound but adds fuel to the fire. It does not prevent the bitterness of this illicit act when committed, but rather makes way for it to be committed freely. In fact, a carnal man in any order fears and is more terrified of being despised in the sight of men than of being condemned at the bar of the supreme Judge. And so he prefers bearing the hardship of any strict penance at any price to being subject to the risk of losing his rank. While he is not afraid of losing the state of his honour through indiscreet discretion, he is encouraged to presume on the untried and

---

[4] Literally "ecclesiastical order."

30

to remain for a long time in what he presumed against his will.[5] I would say that as long as he is not borne away to where he will suffer more severely, he continues to wallow voluptuously in the pigsty of foul obscenity into which he had fallen earlier.

[5] I am not sure what this sentence means. "The untried" seems to refer to remaining an ecclesiastic even after a serious sexual offence; "against his will" suggests that the presumption is more a result of the encouragement of lax superiors and of the offender's fears than of his informed choice.

III

THOSE GIVEN OVER TO UNCLEAN ACTS SHOULD NOT BE PROMOTED TO ORDERS, AND THOSE ALREADY PROMOTED SHOULD NOT REMAIN IN ORDERS

It seems utterly preposterous to us that those who are habitually defiled with this festering contagion would dare either to be promoted to orders or to remain in their rank if already promoted since it is proved to be contrary to reason and against the canonical decrees of the fathers. However, I do not make this claim as though I were offering a definitively decisive judgment in the presence of your majesty, but simply in order to make my own opinion known.

In fact, this shameful act is not improperly believed to be worse than all other crimes since, indeed, we read that almighty God always dealt with this detested evil in one way. Even before he had placed the bridle of legal precept on the other vices, he was already censuring it with the punishment of a severe penalty. There is no need to mention that he destroyed the two famous cities of Sodom and Gomorrah and all their surrounding regions by sulphur and fire from heaven.[6] Scripture attests that he struck down Onan, the son of Judah, with premature death for this nefarious crime, "Onan knew that the descendants would not be counted as his, so whenever he had relations with his brother's wife, he wasted his seed on the ground in order that children not be born in the

[6] See Gen. 19.

32

name of his brother. And for this the Lord killed him, because he had done a detestable thing."[7] It is also written in the Law, "If a man lies with a male as with a woman, both of them have done evil and shall be put to death; their blood will be upon them."[8]

Moreover, blessed Pope Gregory testifies to the fact that a man who has fallen into that crime which the Old Law commands to be condemned by death must not be promoted to ecclesiastical orders. In his letters he writes to Bishop Passivus, saying:

> Your fraternity has known well for how long a time Aprutium has been without pastoral care while we searched unsuccessfully for someone worthy of ordination. But because Importunus is reported to me as having conducted his life consistent with his moral principles and is praised for his zeal in psalm-singing and his love of prayer, we wish that your fraternity have this man present himself to you, and that you discover from [an examination of] his soul how far he has advanced in good deeds. And if no faults are found in him which stand in the way as items punishable by death under the rule of sacred Law, let him be ordained[9] by you as either a monk or subdeacon. After a further period of time, if it please God, let him be promoted to the pastoral care.[10]

So from this we clearly gather that any male who falls into sin with a male—into that crime, as we showed above, which is surely to be punished by death in the judgment of the Old Law—even if he burns with the zeal of psalm-singing, and is distinguished in his love of prayer, and leads a full religious life under a witness of approved reputation, can indeed receive full pardon for his offence, but he is never permitted to aspire to ecclesiastical orders. For even though that venerable man Importunus—marked with the badge of such a reli-

---

[7] Gen. 38:9-10. The point here seems to be that Onan's contraceptive act was as "unnatural" as homosexual acts since both were punished with death.

[8] Lev. 20:13.

[9] Damian's text here reads "ordinandus est" = "to be ordained" (PL 145, 163A) and is repeated a little further on. The text of John the Deacon's *Life of Gregory* reads "hortandus" = "to be exhorted" (PL 75, 137B). The critical text of the letters of Pope Gregory I reads "tonsorandus" and gives the variants, "orandus" and "hortandus" (ed. by L. Hartmann, *Gregorii I registrum epistolarum*, MGH, Epistolae 2, 305). "Ordinandus" seems the least suitable reading, but its repetition later suggests that it was in the text Damian had at hand.

[10] John the Deacon, *Life of Gregory* (PL 75, 137B); see Ryan, *Damiani* (28, text 16).

gious and upright life and decorated with the glories of the virtues—is first extolled with so much fervent praise, afterwards it is said of him, "If no crimes which are punishable by death under the rule of sacred Law stand in the way,[11] he is to be ordained."

Surely it is clear that a person who has been degraded by a crime deserving death is not reformed so as to receive an order of ecclesiastical rank by any sort of subsequent religious life. Nor can one who has certainly fallen into the pit of a mortal fault rise to receive the highest of honours. Consequently, it is clearer than light that whoever is convicted of having fallen in the aforesaid manner—which undoubtedly is a mortal crime—that person is promoted to an ecclesiastical rank entirely against the norm of sacred Law and the rule of divine authority.

[11] "Stand in the way" translates "obviant" in the original quotation above. However, Damian changes the verb in this repetition to "obiiciant," which has the same sense as the original.

IV

WHETHER SUCH SHOULD BE ALLOWED TO FUNCTION IN THIS OFFICE IN THE EVENT OF ECCLESIASTICAL NEED

But perhaps someone will say, "There is an imminent necessity and there is no one to perform a sacred function in the church. The judgment which was first based on the pronouncement of divine justice is reasonably modified by the proposed necessity of the situation."

To this I reply briefly. Did not necessity also weigh heavily when the Papal See lacked a shepherd? Will a judgment be owed in favour of one man which, if upheld, will result in the destitution of a whole people? Will what is not relaxed for the benefit of an immense multitude be violated for the benefit of a single person? But now let the great preacher himself also come forward and let what he thinks of this vice be more expressly known. He says in the Epistle to the Ephesians, "Make no mistake about this: no fornicator, no unclean or covetous person has any inheritance in the kingdom of Christ and of God."[12] Consequently, if an unclean man has no inheritance at all in heaven, by what presumption, by what rash pride should he continue to possess a dignity in the Church which is no less the Kingdom of God?[13] Surely, one who disregards the divine law by falling into sin will not dare to defy it by ascending even to the office of ecclesiastical dignity. Fur-

[12] Eph. 5:5.
[13] See Damian, Opusc. 17 (PL 145, 386A) for a similar comment on Eph. 5:5.

35

thermore, he saves nothing for himself, because he is not afraid of defying God in everything.

Indeed, this Law was enacted particularly for those who violated it as Paul attests when writing to Timothy, saying, "The Law is not made for the just, but for the unjust, for the irreligious and the sinful, for criminals and the defiled, for those who kill their fathers and their mothers, for murderers, for fornicators, for male bed-companions, for kidnappers, for liars, for perjurers, and those who in other ways flout sound teaching."[14] Since it is clear that the Law was passed for male bed-companions so that they would not dare desecrate the sacred orders, by whom, I ask, will the law be kept if it is defied particularly by those for whom it was enacted?

Even if a person is perhaps said to be useful, it is right that the care with which he obeys the authentically sanctioned commands should be in proportion to the prudence he shows in living up to his natural talents. The better anyone's knowledge is, the worse is his sin, since the person who could have prudently avoided sin if he wished will inevitably merit punishment. As blessed James says, "When a man knows the right thing to do and does not do it, he sins."[15] And Truth says, "When more has been given a man, more will be required of him."[16] If the right order of ecclesiastical discipline is confused in a learned man, it is a wonder it is kept by the ignorant. If one of the learned is admitted improperly to an ecclesiastical order, he seems, as it were, to offer his followers and, I might say, to the more simple, the path of error which he himself approached to tread with the swollen foot of pride.[17] Nor must he be judged solely because he sinned, but also because he invited others to emulate the sinning by the example of his own presumption.

[14] 1 Tim. 1:9-10.
[15] James 4:17.
[16] See Luke 12:48.
[17] See Ps. 36:12.

V

THOSE WHO DESIRE TO HAVE SACRED ORDERS AFTER THIS VICE HAVE FALLEN INTO A DEPRAVED SENSE

For who would turn a deaf ear; yes, who would not tremble to the core when he hears the Apostle, as a thundering trumpet, say of such men, "God delivered them up in the desires of their heart to unclean practices; they engaged in the mutual degradation of their bodies?"[18] And a little further on:

> God therefore delivered them up to disgraceful passions. For their women exchanged natural intercourse for unnatural, and in like manner the men gave up natural intercourse with women and burned with lust for one another. Men did shameful things with men, and thus received in their own persons the fitting recompense for their perversity. They did not see fit to acknowledge God, so God delivered them up to their own depraved sense to do what is unseemly.[19]

Now why do they so fervently seek the sublime height of ecclesiastical orders after such a grave fall? What is one to think; what is one to believe but that God has delivered them over to a depraved sense? And because of their sins he does not permit them to see what is necessary for them. Because the sun sets on them, that is, the sun which rises above the heavens,[20] after having lost their interior eyes they are

[18] Rom. 1:24.
[19] Rom. 1:26-28.
[20] See Ps. 67:5 (Vulgate).

completely unable to consider the gravity of the evils which they commit through impurity. Nor are they able to consider the evil of what they inordinately desire against the will of God. It is the usual result of the rule of divine justice that those who defile themselves with the most ruinous filth are struck by a judgment of deserved punishment and incur the shades of blindness. As we read of the ancient authors of this foulness:

> With that, they pressed hard against Lot, moving in closer to break down the door. But (says Scripture) the men put out their hands, pulled Lot inside with them, and closed the door; at the same time they struck the men at the entrance, from the least to the greatest, with such a blindness that they were unable to find the doorway.[21]

Moreover, it is clearly not incongruous to see the persons of the Father and the Son signified by those two angels who, we read, came to blessed Lot. This is apparent from what Lot himself says to them, "O no my Lord! Surely your servant has found favour with you and great is the mercy which you have shown me in saving my life."[22] For it is certain that Lot spoke to the two in the singular as if to one since he worshipped one substance in two persons.

So Sodomites try to break in violently on the angels when unclean men attempt to approach God through the offices of sacred orders. But these latter are surely struck with blindness because they fall into such interior darkness through a just judgment of God that they are powerless to find the door. Divided from God by sin, they do not know how to return to him from that condition. For it is obvious that those who desire to approach God by the routes of arrogance and pride and not by the route of humility do not recognize where the entrance is, or that the door is Christ, as he himself says, "I am the door."[23] Those who lose Christ because of sins cannot find the door, like those who were unable to enter the dwelling of the heavenly citizens. Consequently, they are delivered over to a depraved sense since, as long as they do not weigh the gravity of their guilt in the balance of their own minds, they think the very heavy leaden mass[24] is the lightness of petty

[21] Gen. 19:9-11. Jerome associates "Sodom" with blindness in *Liber de nominibus Hebraicis* (PL 23, 828, "Sodona").

[22] Gen. 19:18-19.

[23] John 10:7.

[24] For "leaden mass" see Zech. 5:8 and Damian, Opusc. 18.2 (PL 145, 412C).

punishments. So what is said there, "They struck the men at the entrance with blindness,"[25] the Apostle clearly declares when he says, "God delivered them up to their own depraved sense."[26] And what is added there, "That they were unable to find the doorway,"[27] he also clearly expresses when he says, "to do what is unseemly."[28] This is as if he were to have said that they try to enter where they ought not.

What else is it for one who is unworthy of an ecclesiastical order to try to break into the office of the sacred altar but to abandon the threshold and to endeavour to enter through the impenetrable barrier of the wall? Because a free passage does not appear for their feet, such men are deceived by their own presumption and are compelled rather to remain in the outer vestibule, while they promise themselves they can reach the sanctuary. Indeed they can strike their foreheads on the rocks of Sacred Scripture, but under no circumstances are they permitted to go in through the entrace granted by divine authority. While they attempt to enter where they are not permitted, they do nothing else but grope vainly at the protected wall. What the prophet says does not unreasonably apply to them, "And at noonday they grope as though it were night."[29] Those who cannot cross the threshold of the proper entrance are turned about, wandering in a circle in whirling madness. Of these the Psalmist says, "My God make them as a wheel."[30] And again, "The wicked walk in a circle."[31] Paul speaks of them a little further on in the passage already cited, "Those who do such things deserve death. And not only those who do them but those who approve them in others."[32]

Clearly, anyone not awakened by such terrible thundering of apostolic invective is correctly judged to be dead, not to be carelessly sleeping. And since the Apostle amplifies the sentence of strict punishment with such zeal, not just for some of the faithful Jews but for pagans and for those who do not know God, what, I ask, would he say if he saw such a wound festering in the very body of the holy Church? In particular, what sadness, what burning compassion would

---

[25] Gen. 19:11.
[26] Rom. 1:28.
[27] Gen. 19:11.
[28] Rom. 1:28.
[29] Job 5:14.
[30] Ps. 83:14 (Vulgate).
[31] Ps. 12:9.
[32] Rom. 1:32.

inflame that pious heart if he were to learn that this destructive plague was even spreading among the sacred orders?

Let the indolent superiors of clerics and of priests hear; let them hear and let them greatly fear being participants in the guilt of others, even though they feel safe as far as they themselves are concerned. I refer to those who close their eyes to the correction of their subordinates' sins and offer them the freedom of sinning through an ill-advised silence. Let them hear, I say, and prudently understand that they all equally deserve death—namely, "not only those who do them but also those who approve them in others.

VI

SPIRITUAL FATHERS WHO ARE DEFILED ALONG WITH THEIR CHILDREN

O unheard of crime! O outrage to be mourned with a whole fountain of tears! If those who consent to the ones doing these things are to be punished with death, what torment could be thought fitting for those who commit these great evils with their spiritual children—evils to be punished with damnation? What fruitfulness can still be found in the flocks when the shepherd is so deeply sunk in the belly of the devil? Who would still remain under the rule of one who, he knew, was separated from God as an enemy? Whoever makes a mistress out of a penitent whom he had spiritually borne as a child for God subjects the servant to the iron rule of diabolical tyranny through the impurity of his flesh. If someone violates a woman whom he raised from the sacred font, is it not determined that he be deprived of communion without delay, and ordered to pass through public penance by censure of the sacred canons?[33] For it is written: spiritual generation is greater than carnal.[34]

Likewise it follows that the same sentence is justly inflicted both on one who has ruined a natural daughter and on one who has corrupted a spiritual daughter through a sacrilegious union, unless perhaps in this

---

[33] Ryan, *Damiani* (29, text 17), suggests that Burchard, *Decretum* 17, 8 (PL 140, 920C), is Damian's source for these remarks.

[34] I am unable to identify the source for this saying. The same expression is used elsewhere by Damian without any suggestion of its being a citation; Opusc. 17 (PL 145, 385A). Perhaps it is a reflection of the Council of Trullo, canon 53 in Mansi 11, 907.

matter the quality of each crime is distinguished, since, although sinning incestuously, nevertheless, they each sinned naturally because they sinned with a woman. However, anyone who commits a sacrilege with his son is guilty of the crime of incest with a male and breaks the laws of nature. And it seems to me to be more tolerable to fall into shameful lust with an animal than with a male.[35] That is, one who perishes alone is judged much more lightly than one who also draws another along with himself to disastrous ruin. In fact, it is a sad situation where the ruin of one person depends in this way on the ruin of another so that while one is destroyed the other necessarily follows to death close behind.

[35] Perhaps an explicit contradiction of the "Second Diocesan Statute" of Theodulf of Orleans which reads, "For just as it is more abominable to mix with a mule than with a male, so it is a more irrational crime to mix with a male than with a female." Edited in C. De Clercq, *La législation religieuse franque de Clovis à Charlemagne* (Louvain, 1936), no. 39, 336 (PL 105, 214D).

VII

THOSE WHO CONFESS THEIR CRIMES TO THE VERY ONES WITH WHOM THEY FELL

However, that the arguments of diabolical fraud might not lie hidden, I will bring into the light what was fashioned secretly in the workshop of ancient wickedness. I do not accept that this hidden thing should go on, namely, that certain ones who are filled with the poison of this crime, as if taking heart, should confess to one another to keep the knowledge of their guilt from becoming known to others. While they shame the face of men, the authors of this guilt themselves become the judges. The indiscreet indulgence which each desires to be applied to himself, he rejoices to bestow on the other through a delegated change of roles. So it happens that although they ought to be penitents for their great crimes, nonetheless their faces do not pale with fasting, nor do their bodies waste away with thinness. While the belly is in no way restrained from the immoderate reception of food, the spirit is shamefully inflamed to the ardour of habitual lust,[36] with the result that the one who had shed no tears for what was committed continues to commit more seriously what should be mourned.

But it is a precept of the Law that when a person is covered with leprosy he be shown to the priests.[37] Now, however, he is shown to the leprous rather than to the priests since the impure confess to the impure

[36] Elsewhere Damian provides a detailed account of the relationship between eating and sexual arousal; see Letter 1.15 (PL 144, 230B-32A).

[37] Lev. 14:2.

the wickedness they committed together.[38] But since confession is also a manifestation, what, I ask, does he manifest who tells the listener what is known; in what way is it to be called a confession where nothing is revealed by the one making the confession except what the listener already knows? Besides, by what law, by what right can he who is bound by the social bond of the evil deed bind or loose the other? Vainly does he strive to loose another while he himself is ensnared in chains. If anyone wishes to be a guide for a blind person, it is necessary that he himself see lest he cause the one following to fall, as the voice of Truth says, "If one blind man guide another, both fall into a pit."[39] And again, "You see the speck in your brother's eye, and yet miss the plank in your own. Hypocrite, remove the plank from your own eye first; then you will see clearly enough to remove the speck from your brother's eye."[40]

It is evident from these Gospel witnesses that those shrouded in the darkness of the same guilt strive in vain to recall each other to the light of penance.[41] And while he is not afraid of perishing by leading another astray beyond his own powers, the one who follows does not escape the pit of present ruin along with him.

[38] The Migne edition (PL 145, 190B-D) adds a comment to this passage, which also applies to what immediately follows, suggesting that Peter Damian is not claiming that the confessions performed by such priests are invalid. The scholion applies particularly to the statement a few sentences later, "Vainly does he strive to loose another while he himself is ensnared in chains." The scholion is probably correct, particularly when we recall the strong defense Damian made of the validity of the ministrations by simoniacal priests in his Opusc. 6, ed. by L. von Heinemann, *Liber gratissimus*, MGH, Libelli de lite I, 15-75, and PL 145, 99-156. See also Opusc. 30 (PL 145, 523A-30C).

[39] See Luke 6:39.

[40] Luke 6:41-42.

[41] Literally, "whoever is shrouded in the darkness of the same guilt strives in vain to recall another to the light of penance."

VIII

JUST AS THE SACRILEGIOUS VIOLATOR OF A VIRGIN, SO ALSO THE PROSTITUTOR OF A SPIRITUAL SON MUST BE DEPOSED BY LAW

Now I meet you face to face, carnal man, whoever you are. Do you ever refuse to confess to spiritual men what you have committed because you fear giving up your ecclesiastical rank? But how much more salutary was it to endure temporary shame in the sight of men, than to be subject to eternal punishment before the tribunal of the supreme Judge? Perhaps you say to me, "If a male falls with a male through femoral fornication only, he should indeed do penance, but in the interests of pious humanity he should not be cast irrevocably from his rank." I ask you: if someone risked acting sacrilegiously with a virgin, will he in your judgment remain in his rank? But you would without doubt judge that such a person be deposed. Therefore, it follows that what you reasonably assert in the case of a consecrated virgin, you must also admit of a spiritual son. So what you seem to assert of spiritual fathers, you must determine equally for clerics. Yet, while maintaining these distinctions, an act is judged to be all the more serious to the extent that it is shown to be against nature because of the identity of the sexes involved. Besides, in law we always turn to the criminal's will when judging excesses; one who pollutes masculine thighs would have done with a male through the insanity of unrestrained lust everything that is done with women if nature had permitted it. He did what was possible, and so, arriving at what nature

45

has denied, he unwillingly fixed the limit of the crime, where the necessity of nature set the unbreachable limit of the faculty.

Therefore, since it is the same law for both sexes,[42] for consecrated men and for clerics, we conclude that just as the sacrilegious violator of a virgin is deposed by the law, so the prostitutor of a spiritual son must also be barred from his [ecclesiastical] office by every means available.

[42] Perhaps an adaptation of the Council of Compiègne (A.D. 757), canon 4, "There is one law for men and for women" (A. Boretius, *Capitularia*, no. 15). See Peter Damian, Opusc. 16 (PL 145, 374B, 375C); Opusc. 18.1 (PL 145, 393A).

IX

THOSE WHO SIN WITH EITHER A NATURAL OR BAPTISMAL DAUGHTER ARE GUILTY OF THE SAME CRIME

To turn the dispute back now to the sacred, that is, to the accursed confessors. If a priest who is a canon has fallen with a woman to whom he had declared a judgment of penance even once, no one doubts that he is to be degraded by the censure of a synodal judgment. Moreover, if a male religious sins with another male religious for whom he was either a judge in giving a penance or by whom he was judged in receiving one, will he not lose the honour of his rank on the basis of a declaration of justice? By popular custom a son through penance is thought of in the same way as a son through baptism. Whence we read that blessed Mark the evangelist was the son of Peter through baptism.[43] The great preacher says, "For Christ did not send me to baptize, but to preach the gospel."[44] He says again: For what is my glory before the Lord; do you not know?[45] "It was I who begot you in Christ Jesus through the gospel."[46] And again to the Galatians he says, "My little children, you put me back in labour pains until Christ is formed in you."[47] It follows from this that, if he who was sent not to baptize but to evangelize and so to proclaim repentance was responsible

[43] 1 Pet. 5:13.
[44] 1 Cor. 1:17.
[45] See 1 Thes. 2:19.
[46] 1 Cor. 4:15.
[47] Gal. 4:19.

for conception and birth, he is rightly called a son who receives a penance, and a father who imposes a penance. Now, if what was said above is carefully attended to, it is clearer than day that a person who fornicates with a natural daughter or with a daughter through baptism as well as a person who acts shamefully with one who is a son through penance are guilty of the same crime. Moreover, it is just that a person who falls into impurity with a son through penance be separated in every way from the order which he administers. This is similar to the case of the person who fell into sin with a daughter whom he had conceived naturally or whom he had received from baptism or on whom he had imposed a judgment of penance.

X

THE APOCRYPHAL CANONS IN WHICH THOSE WHO TRUST ARE COMPLETELY DECEIVED

Since in the sacred canons there are some sad things discovered in which lost men trust in vain presumption, we add some of them here to demonstrate clearly that not only they but all others like them are false and entirely apocryphal, wherever they might be found. For among other things it is said:

(1) "A priest without the vow of a monk who sins with a young girl or a prostitute shall do penance for two years, and during the three lents, on Monday, Wednesday, Friday, and Saturday, always on dry bread."[48]

(2) "If with a female servant of God or with a male, a fast is added, that is, five years if it is habitual."[49]

(3) "Similarly deacons, if they are not monks, two years, just like monks who are without rank."[50]

[48] See Ryan, *Damiani* (29, text 18), for Damian's immediate source in Burchard, *Decretum* 17. 39 (PL 140, 926C-27D). Burchard's text resembles the *Penitential of Egbert* but is most probably from a text belonging to the same family as the penitential edited by B. Albers in "Wann sind die Beda-Egbert'schen Bussbücher verfasst worden und wer ist ihr Verfasser?," *Archiv für katholisches Kirchenrecht* 81 (1901), 393-420 (see pp. 407-409). In the penitential selections which follow I simply note the reference in Burchard and point out any divergence in Damian's text from Burchard as printed in PL 140. In the present selection Burchard's penance is three years and he has "dry food" while Damian has "dry bread."

[49] See Burchard, 17.39 (PL 140, 926D), "seven years."

[50] See Burchard, 17.39 (PL 140, 926C).

A little further on it is added:

(4) "A cleric without the vow of a monk who fornicates with a young girl shall do penance for half a year; likewise if he is a canon; if frequently, for two years."[51]

(5) "Again, if anyone has sinned as the Sodomites, some say ten years penance; if he is in the habit, more must be added; if he has ecclesiastical rank, he is to be degraded and do penance as a lay person."[52]

(6) "A man who commits femoral fornication shall do penance for one year; if he repeats it, two years."[53]

(7) "However, if he commits anal fornication, he shall do penance for three years; if he is a boy, two years."[54]

(8) "If he fornicates with an animal or a mule he shall do penance for ten years."[55]

(9) "Again a bishop sinning with an animal shall do penance for ten years and lose his rank; a priest, five years; a deacon, three years; a cleric, two years."[56]

Many other deceptive and sacrilegious items are found inserted in the sacred canons through the wiles of the devil which we are more willing to erase than to write down, more ready to spit upon than to impress such vain derisions on paper. But see, carnal men trust in this nonsense; they believe in them as though in the portents of dreams and delude themselves in the security of a vain hope. However, let us see whether they agree with canonical authority and whether I might learn if they are to be upheld or avoided, not so much in words as in attesting deeds.

---

[51] Damian differs considerably from Burchard here. See Burchard, 17.39 (PL 140, 926D): "A cleric without the vow of a monk, if he fornicates with such a young girl, shall do penance for one year; if frequently, for two years. If with a canoness, for two years; if frequently, for three years."

[52] See Burchard, 17.39 (PL140, 926D).

[53] Ibid. (PL 140, 927A).

[54] Ibid.

[55] Ibid.

[56] Ibid.

XI

A CREDIBLE REFUTATION OF THE AFORESAID CANONS

Let us return to the beginning of that fallacious chapter which reads: (1) "A priest without the vow of a monk who sins with a young girl or a prostitute shall do penance for two years." Now who is so dull, who can be found so insane as to believe that a priest caught in fornication should receive a penance worth two years? Anyone who has even a minimal knowledge of canonical authority or a superior knowledge (we can be silent about the stricter judgments), knows clearly that a priest who has fallen into fornication is judged to be deserving of at least ten years penance.[57] Moreover, this penance of two years for fornication not only is not to be applied to priests, but not even to lay persons, for the judgment is three years when they turn away from this ruin to satisfaction. Then it is added: (2) If he sins "with a female servant of God or with a male (understood to be a priest), a fast is added, that is, of five years if it is habitual." (3) "Similarly deacons, if they are not monks, shall do penance for two years just like monks who are without rank."

One thing I see at once at the head of this senseless opinion which I am exposing and I gladly take note of it. Undoubtedly it says, (2) "If with a female servant of God or with a male." See, O good Sodomite man, in your own scripture which you singularly love, which you eagerly love, which you fasten to yourself as a shield of defence, see before your own eyes that it makes no difference whether one sins with

[57] See Burchard, 17.56 (PL 140, 931D).

a female servant of God or with a male. Equal sins are believed to be judged equally. Now, there is nothing to fight about with me in this, . nothing you can rightly dissent from in my allegations. But who is so madly insane, who is in such dark and profound blindness that he would think a penance of five years is to be imposed on a priest for sinning with a female servant of God, that is, with a nun, or two years on a deacon or a monk? Is this not an insidious snare for those on the road to destruction? Is this not a snare for erring souls?

Who could not give the lie to what is said: (4) "A cleric without the vow of a monk who fornicates with a young girl shall do penance for half a year"? And who is so versed in the knowledge of sacred scripture, so keen with the sharpness of dialectical subtlety, that he can both presume to condemn the law with [another] law and put forward as praiseworthy what can be adjuged to be the prejudice of a detestable authority? Why is three years given to a lay man while a cleric is ordered to do penance for half a year? So the blessed clerics who fornicate, if judged by the judgment of sodomists, in fact mete out to others in the same measure that they desire to be measured themselves. The greedy author of this error is satisfied to win souls for the devil and while he is zealous to destroy monks, he extends his perverse teaching to the order of clerics. While the murderer of souls was not able to satisfy the stomach's gluttony for malice with the death of monks alone, he desired to satiate himself from another order.

Now let us see what follows: (5) "If anyone has sinned as the Sodomites, some say ten years of penance; if he is in the habit, more must be added; if he has ecclesiastical rank he is to be degraded, and do penance as a lay person." (7) "A man who commits femoral fornication shall do penance for one year; if he repeats it, two years." (8) "However, if he commits anal fornication he shall do penance for three years." And since to sin as the Sodomites do, as you yourself advance, is none other than to perform anal fornication, why is it that your canons are found to contain in only one statement such differences and variations, so that they enjoin the weight of ten years on those who sin as Sodomites, but for anal fornicators, which is the same, they reduce the lament of penance to the brevity of three years?

Are these not deservedly to be compared to monsters, not monsters resulting from nature but made by human industry, some of which begin with horses' heads and end with goats' hooves? With what canons, with what decrees of the fathers do these mockeries agree which are mutually discordant as well as being echoes from a horned brow?[58] Are they not at variance with themselves? By what authorities . are they supported? The Saviour says, "For every kingdom divided against itself is laid waste, and house will fall upon house. If Satan is divided against himself, how will his teaching stand?"[59] At one time they seem to intend a severe judgment, at another to exhibit a kind of cruel mercy, and as with a chimerical monster which looks like a lion, here he emits terrible threats, there he humbly blesses the head of the evildoer. These different versions excite to laughter rather than join together in the lament of penance.

The following are in similar error: (8) "He who fornicates with an animal or a mule shall do penance for ten years." (9) "Again, a bishop sinning with animals shall do penance for ten years and lose his rank; a priest, five years; a deacon, three; a cleric, two." Since it first says unconditionally: whoever fornicates with an animal or a mule will be punished with ten years satisfaction, how does what is added follow: that the penance to be imposed for intercourse with animals is to be five years for a priest, three for a deacon, two for a cleric? So any layman, whoever he is, is afflicted with punishment for a period of ten years, while five is imposed on a priest, that is, a half of the whole penance is relaxed. With what pages of the sacred canons, I ask, do these silly dreams agree which are so clearly at variance with themselves? Who will not think, who will not see clearly that these and similar canons are diabolical creations, instituted to deceive the souls of the simple through cunning fraud?

For just as poison is deceptively mixed in honey or other tasty foods so that, while the delicacy of the food invites to eat, the hidden poison is more easily spread throughout the interior of the man, likewise,

---

[58] Perhaps "horned brow" may be a reference to sophistical forms of argument; see St. Jerome, Letter 69 to Oceanus in *Sancti Eusebii Hieronymi epistolae*, ed. by I. Hilberg (Corpus scriptorum ecclesiasticorum latinorum, 54; Vienna, 1910), 680; *Commentariorum in Matheum libri IV*, ed. by D. Hurst and M. Adriaen (Corpus christianorum, series latina, 7; Turnhout, 1969); *De perpetua virginitate B. Mariae adversus Helvidium* (PL 23, 210B); and Martianus Capella, *De nuptiis philologiae et Mercurii libri VIIII* in *Martianus Capella*, ed. by A. Dick, revised by J. Preaux (Stuttgart, 1969), 327, translated in, *Martianus Capella and the Seven Liberal Arts*, Vol. 2, *The Marriage of Philology and Mercury*, trans. by W. H. Stahl and R. Johnsen with F. L. Burge (Records of Civilization: Sources and Studies, 84; New York, 1977), 106.

[59] Luke 11:17-18.

these cunning and deceptive commentaries are inserted into the sacred writings to avoid the suspicion of falsity. And they are besmeared as with a certain honey, while they seem to be seasoned with the sweetness of a false piety. Beware of them, whoever you are, lest the song of the Sirens soften you with death-dealing sweetness, lest it drown the ship of your mind in the depths of Scylla's whirlpool. The open sea of the sacred councils should not terrify you with its express austerity; the shallow sand banks of the apocryphal canons should not betray you by the enticing calmness of the waves. While fleeing the tumultuous waves a ship often experiences shipwreck when approaching the sandy shores; and often it has gotten safely to shore without throwing the cargo overboard while sailing over the depths of the sea.

XII

THESE MOCKERIES ARE TO BE EXCLUDED FROM THE SACRED CANONS SINCE THEY DO NOT SEEM TO HAVE CERTAIN AUTHORSHIP[60]

Indeed, who fashioned these canons? Who presumed to plant such thorns in the noble grove of the Church—such prickly, thorny thistles? It is clear beyond any doubt that all authentic canons either were arrived at in venerable synodal councils or were promulgated by the holy fathers, pontiffs of the Apostolic See. Nor is any single individual permitted to publish canons; this privilege belongs to him alone who is seen presiding in the chair of blessed Peter. However, these spurious offshoots of canons of which we are speaking are known to be excluded by the sacred councils,[61] and are proved to be altogether foreign to the decrees of the fathers. Therefore, it follows that they should never find a place among the canons since they are seen to proceed neither from the decretal pronouncements of the fathers nor from the sacred councils. Whatever is not included among the species is undoubtedly foreign to the genus. If the name of the author is asked for, one cannot answer with certainty since it cannot be uniformly found in the

[60] A translation of this chapter may be found in O. D. Watkins, *A History of Penance: Being a Study of the Authorities*, Vol. 2 (London, 1920), 740-41; it is partially translated in J. T. McNeill and H. M. Gamer, *Medieval Handbooks of Penance*, 411.

[61] The penitentials in general were condemned by two early ninth-century councils, Chalon (A.D. 813), canon 38 and Paris (A. D. 829), canon 32. For translations of these canons see J. T. McNeill and H. Gamer, *Handbooks*, 401-403.

codices. In one place it is written, "Theodore says," in another, "the Roman Penitential says," in another, "the Canons of the Apostles." Some are entitled in one way, some in another, and since they do not deserve to have a single author, without doubt they lose all authority.[62] Canons which waver under so many unascertained authors confirm none with certain authority; and what generates the mist of doubt for readers must yield after the light of sacred writings has removed all doubts.

Now, indeed, with this theatrical madness upon which carnal men presumed eliminated from the number of the canons and convicted by the clarity of rational argument, we shall present those canons whose trustworthiness and authenticity we in no way doubt. In fact they are found in the Council of Ancyra.

[62] See Burchard, 17.39 (PL 140, 926B-D), Ryan, *Damiani* (30, text 20). In this passage Burchard also mentions Bede. Perhaps Peter Damian omitted the reference to Bede since he uses him later as an authority.

XIII

"THOSE WHO FORNICATE IRRATIONALLY, THAT IS, WHO MIX WITH CATTLE OR WHO ARE POLLUTED WITH MALES"

Of those who have acted or who act irrationally: as often as they have committed such a crime before the age of twenty, after fifteen years of penance they should merit the community of prayers; then, after spending five years in this community, they can have the eucharist. However, the quality of their lives is to be discussed during the time of penance, and so they might obtain mercy. And if they are given insatiably to these heretical crimes they are to undertake to do penance for a longer time. However, if this is done after age twenty by those who are married, after twenty-five years of penance they will be received into the community of prayers in which they remain for five years and then they can receive the eucharist. If they are married and over fifty and fall into this sin they can receive the grace of communion at the end of their lives.[63]

Look! in the very title of this venerable authority we see that not only those who fall by consummating the act against nature but also those

[63] Council of Ancyra, canon 16 (PL 67, 154C), see Ryan, *Damiani* (30, text 21); Bailey, *Homosexuality*, 86-89 discusses this canon; see also Boswell, *Homosexuality*, 178. For a discussion of the grades of penitents mentioned in this canon see Watkins, *History of Penance* 2, 285-86.

who are polluted in any way with males are compared primarily with those who lie with cattle. For if we pay attention to the interjected expressions, we see the issue proposed with the balance of great discernment when it says, "Those who mix with cattle or who are polluted with males." For if by the words, "those who are polluted with males" it wanted to signify only those who sin against nature through a consummated act, it would not have been necessary for it to use two terms since the term "mixed" alone could have expressed its meaning. In fact, for brevity of style it would have been enough if the whole judgment had been encompassed in one expression saying, "Those who mix with cattle or males," since those who violate cattle or males mix in the same way. For although it says some "mix" with cattle and others do not mix but "are polluted" with males, it is quite clear that in the end of the expression a sentence is imposed not only on the corruptors of males but on those who pollute in any way whatsoever.

Moreover, it should be noted that the edict of this constitution was instituted principally for lay people. This is easily inferred from what is added in the following, "If this is done after age twenty by those who are married, after twenty-five years of penance they will be received into the community of prayers in which they remain for five years and then they can receive the eucharist." Therefore, if a secular person who is guilty of this outrage is admitted to the community of prayers after spending twenty-five years in penance, but yet is not admitted to receive the eucharist, for what reason can a religious man be judged worthy not only to receive but even to offer and to consecrate the sacred mysteries themselves? If a lay person is scarcely permitted to enter a church to pray with others, how is it granted to a religious to approach the altar to intercede for others? If a lay person, before he completes such a long period of penance does not merit to be a hearer, how is a religious worthy to celebrate the sacred solemnity of the mass? If the lay person who sinned less is unworthy to receive into his mouth the gift of the heavenly eucharist if he repeats the act over the course of time, how will the religious merit to handle such an awesome mystery with polluted hands?

Now let us see what the same Council of Ancyra has defined for the same crime.

XIV

"THOSE WHO WERE ONCE POLLUTED WITH ANIMALS OR MALES, OR WHO STILL LANGUISH IN THIS VICE"

"The holy synod commands that those who have lived irrationally and who have polluted others with the leprosy of this unjust crime are to pray among those who are struck with an unclean spirit."[64] Clearly, while it does not say, "who corrupt others with the leprosy of this unjust crime," but "pollute" which, however, corresponds to the title where it begins with those polluted but not corrupted, it is clear that in whatever way a male is polluted with a male through lustful ardour, he is commanded to pray among the demoniacs and not among Christian Catholics. And so if carnal men do not know how to realize what they are from one another, at least they can be instructed by those with whom they are relegated in the common penitentiary of prayer.

It is just enough that those who commit their flesh to the demons through such filthy intercourse against the law of nature and the order of human reason be allotted the common nook of prayer along with demoniacs. For inasmuch as human nature itself completely rejects these evils and stands opposed to there being any incompatibility between the sexes, it is clearer than day that these men would never presume to do such strange things to which they were disinclined

---

[64] Council of Ancyra, canon 17 (PL 67, 154D); see Ryan, *Damiani* (31, text 22). The original Ancyra canons 16 and 17 are translated in K. J. Hefele, *A History of the Christian Councils from the Original Documents to the Close of the Council of Nicaea, A. D. 325*, trans. by W. R. Clark (Edinburgh, 1894), 215-17.

unless evil spirits possessed them fully as if they were "vessels fit for wrath, ready to be destroyed."[65] But when they begin to take possession of them, the evil spirits pour the infernal poison of their evil throughout the whole possessed heart which they fill so that the possessed eagerly desire not what the natural motion of the flesh urgently demands, but what diabolical precipitation offers. When a male rushes to a male to commit impurity, this is not the natural impulse of the flesh, but only the goad of diabolical impulse. This is why the holy fathers carefully established that sodomists pray together with the deranged since they did not doubt that the sodomists were possessed by the same diabolical spirit. So how can one who is separated from the congregation of the whole people and commanded to pray only among the demoniacs assist as mediator between God and the people through the dignity of the priestly office?

However, since we have taken care to use two testimonies from one sacred council, let us also insert what Basil the Great thinks of the vice under discussion so that "on the testimony of two or three witnesses every word shall be established."[66] He says:

[65] See Rom. 9:22.
[66] See Deut. 19:15; 2 Cor. 13:1; Burchard, 7.17 (PL 140, 782C).

XV

CLERICS OR MONKS WHO ARE SEDUCERS OF MALES

A cleric or monk who seduces youths or young boys or is found kissing or in any other impure situations is to be publicly flogged and lose his tonsure. When his hair has been shorn, his face is to be foully besmeared with spit and he is to be bound in iron chains. For six months he will languish in prison-like confinement and on three days of each week shall fast on barley bread in the evening. After this he will spend another six months under the custodial care of a spiritual elder, remaining in a segregated cell, giving himself to manual work and prayer, subject to vigils and prayers. He may go for walks but always under the custodial care of two spiritual brethren, and he shall never again associate with youths in private conversation nor in counselling them.[67]

This carnal man whom the sacred authority judges to be degraded by such ignominies and with such awesome reproach should carefully consider whether he can safely administer the ecclesiastical duties. Nor should he flatter himself on not having corrupted anyone else since he should see it clearly written that whoever is found in a kiss alone or in any impure situation will be justly subjected to the whole range of ignominious discipline. And if a kiss is so severely punished, what

---

[67] See Ryan, *Damiani* (31, text 23). The text is from *Regula Fructuosi*, ch. 16 (PL 87, 1107A). English translation, C. W. Barlow, *Rule for the Monastery of Compludo*, in The Fathers of the Church, 63 (Washington, DC, 1969), 169.

should contamination with another merit? To punish this crime, this enormous crime, is it not enough to be whipped in public, to lose his tonsure, to be shamefully shaven, to be smeared with spit, to be cruelly imprisoned for a long time, and to be bound in iron chains besides? Yet finally he is also ordered to be struck with a fast of barley bread since it is right that whoever acts like a horse and a mule[68] not eat the food of men but is to feed on the grain of mules.

In fact, if we neglect to consider the gravity of this sin, it is at least clearly expressed in the very judgment of penance which is imposed. For whoever is bound by canonical censure to submit to public penance is surely judged unworthy of ecclesiastical offices by the wise judgment of the fathers. For this reason blessed Pope Siricius wrote, among other things, saying, "It is right that we should rule that even as no member of the clergy is admitted to penance, so too no layman after penance and reconciliation may obtain the honour of clerical office. For although such men have been cleansed from the stain of all their sins, they still ought not to take up the implements for administering the sacraments after having once themselves been the vessels of vice."[69]

Therefore, since blessed Basil commands those guilty of this crime to undergo not only hard but also public penance, and Siricius forbids a penitent from obtaining clerical orders, we can clearly gather that one who is polluted with a male by the filthy stain of sexual impurity does not merit to perform ecclesiastical duties. Nor are those who were once the vessels of vice worthy to handle the divine mystery, as was said.

[68] See Ps. 32:9.
[69] See Ryan, *Damiani* (31, text 24). English translation in James T. Shotwell and Louise R. Loomis, *The See of Peter* (Records of Civilization: Sources and Studies; New York, 1927), Appendix 1, 706. The prohibition of penance for the clergy mentioned here is the prohibition of *public* penance.

XVI

A DESERVING CONDEMNATION OF
ABOMINABLE SHAMEFULNESS

Truly, this vice is never to be compared with any other vice because it surpasses the enormity of all vices. Indeed, this vice is the death of bodies, the destruction of souls. It pollutes the flesh; it extinguishes the light of the mind. It evicts the Holy Spirit from the temple of the human heart; it introduces the devil who incites to lust. It casts into error; it completely removes the truth from the mind that has been deceived. It prepares snares for those entering; it shuts up those who fall into the pit so they cannot get out. It opens hell; it closes the door of heaven. It makes a citizen of the heavenly Jerusalem into an heir of infernal Babylon. It makes of the star of heaven the stubble of eternal fire; it cuts off a member of the Church and casts it into the consuming fire of boiling Gehenna. This vice tries to overturn the walls of the heavenly homeland and is busy repairing the renewed bulwarks of Sodom. For it is this which violates sobriety, kills modesty, strangles chastity, and butchers irreparable virginity with the dagger of unclean contagion. It defiles everything, stains everything, pollutes everything. And as for itself, it permits nothing pure, nothing clean, nothing other than filth. "To the clean all things are clean, but to the defiled unbelievers nothing is clean."[70]

This vice casts men from the choir of the ecclesiastical community and compels them to pray with the possessed and with those who work for the devil. It separates the soul from God to join it with devils. This

[70] Tit. 1:15.

most pestilential queen of the sodomists makes the followers of her tyrannical laws filthy to men and hateful to God. She commands to join in evil wars against God, to carry the military burden of a most evil spirit. She separates from the companionship of angels and captures the unhappy soul under the yoke of her domination away from its nobility. She deprives her soldiers of the arms[71] of the virtues and exposes them to the piercing spears of all the vices. She humiliates in church, condemns in law, defiles in secret, shames in public, gnaws the conscience as though with worms, sears the flesh as though with fire.

She pants to satisfy her desire for pleasure, but on the other hand she fears lest she become exposed and come out in public and become known to men. Should he not fear her, he who dreads with anxious suspicion the very participant in their common ruin? A person who himself participates in a sinful act ought not to be a judge of the crime in confession as long as he hesitates in any way to confess that he has sinned himself by joining in the sin of another. The fact is that the one partner could not die in sin without the other dying also; nor can one provide an opportunity for the other to rise without rising himself. The miserable flesh burns with the heat of lust; the cold mind trembles with the rancour of suspicion; and in the heart of the miserable man chaos boils like Tartarus, while as often as he is pierced with mental stings he is tormented in a certain measure with painful punishment. In fact, after this most poisonous serpent once sinks its fangs into the unhappy soul, sense is snatched away, memory is borne off, the sharpness of the mind is obscured. It becomes unmindful of God and even forgetful of itself. This plague undermines the foundation of faith, weakens the strength of hope, destroys the bond of charity; it takes away justice, subverts fortitude, banishes temperance, blunts the keenness of prudence.

And what more should I say since it expels the whole host of the virtues from the chamber of the human heart and introduces every barbarous vice as if the bolts of the doors were pulled out. To be sure, the view of Jeremiah which concerns the earthy Jerusalem is suitably adapted to this case, "The foe stretched out his hand to all her treasures; she has seen those nations enter her sanctuary whom you forbade to come into your assembly."[72]

[71] Perhaps an echo of Caesar, *The Gallic War* 3.6.3, trans. by H. J. Edwards (Loeb Classical Library; Cambridge, MA, 1917).

[72] Lam. 1:10.

Indeed, whomever this most atrocious beast once seizes upon with bloodthirsty jaws, it restrains with its bonds from every form of good work and immediately unleashes him down the steep descent of the most evil depravity. In fact, when one has fallen into this abyss of extreme ruin he becomes an exile from the heavenly homeland, separated from the body of Christ, confounded by the authority of the whole Church, condemned by the judgment of all the holy fathers. He is despised among men on earth and rejected from the community of heavenly citizens. Heaven becomes like iron for him and the earth like bronze.[73] Burdened with the weight of the crime, he cannot arise nor conceal his evil for long in the hiding-place of ignorance. He cannot rejoice here while he lives nor can he hope there when he dies, since he is compelled to bear the disgrace of human derision now and afterwards the torment of eternal damnation. The lamentation of the prophet clearly applies to this soul, "Look O Lord, upon my distress: my stomach is in ferment, my heart recoils within me because I am full of bitterness: the sword kills without, and at home death is similar."[74]

[73] Lev. 26:19.
[74] Lam. 1:20.

XVII

A MOURNFUL LAMENT FOR THE SOUL WHO IS GIVEN OVER TO THE FILTH OF IMPURITY[75]

O, I weep for you unfortunate soul, and from the depths of my heart I sigh over the lot of your destruction. I weep for you, I say, miserable soul who are given over to the filth of impurity. You are to be mourned indeed with a whole fountain of tears. What a pity! "Who will give to my head waters and my eyes a fountain of tears?"[76] And this mournful voice is not now less suitably drawn from my sobbing self than was then spoken out of the prophetic mouth. I do not bewail the stone ramparts of a city fortified with towers, not the lower buildings of a temple made by hands; I do not lament the progress of a vile people taken into the captivity of the rule of the Babylonian king. My plaint is for the noble soul made in the image and likeness of God and joined with the most precious blood of Christ. It is brighter than many buildings, certainly to be preferred to all the heights of earthly construction. Therefore I especially lament the lapse of the soul and the destruction of the temple in which Christ had resided. O eyes wear yourselves out in crying aloud, overflow the rivers full of tears, water with continuous tears my sad, mournful face! With the prophet, "let my eyes stream with tears

---

[75] Sections of chapters, 17, 18, and 23 may be found in an Italian translation in C. Mazzotti, "Il celibato e la castità del clero in S. Pier Damiano," *Studi su S. Pier Damiano in onore del Cardinale Amleto Giovanni Cicognani* (2nd ed.; Faenza, 1970), 352-54.

[76] Jer. 8:20.

day and night and not be silent since with a great sorrow the virgin daughter of my people is contrite over her incurable wound."[77] In fact the daughter of my people was struck with the worst blow because the soul, which was the daughter of holy Church, was cruelly wounded with the spear of impurity by the enemy of the human race. She who was nourished tenderly and softly with the milk of sacred teaching in the hall of the eternal King now is infected as by a plague with the poison of lust, buried in the sulphurous ashes of Gomorrah, and is seen lying out rigid. "Those accustomed to dainty food perish in the streets; those brought up in purple now cling to a dung heap."[78] Why? The prophet continues, saying, "For the punishment of the daughter of my people is greater than the penalty of Sodom, which was overthrown in an instant."[79]

In fact, the iniquity of a Christian soul surpasses the sin of the Sodomites because each one now falls in a worse way insofar as he defies the very commands of evangelical grace. The knowledge of divine law vehemently accuses him, lest he find relief in a plan to excuse himself.

Alas! Alas! why, unhappy soul, do you not consider from what heights of dignity you have been cast, and of how much charming splendour and glory you have been stripped? "How the Lord in his wrath covered daughter Zion with darkness. He has cast down from heaven to earth the glory of Israel."[80] "Gone from daughter Zion is all her beauty."[81] I sympathize with your calamity and weep bitterly over your shame, saying, "Worn out from weeping are my eyes, within me all is in ferment; my gall is poured out on the ground because of the downfall of the daughter of my people."[82] And you, pretending to take thought of your wickedness, and yet acquiring souls through crime,[83] say, "I sit enthroned as a queen, no widow am I."[84] Saddened at your captivity I exclaim, "Why is Jacob led away as a slave by birth and Israel become booty?"[85] "You keep saying: I am rich and have grown

---

[77] Jer. 14:17.
[78] Lam. 4:5.
[79] Lam. 4:6.
[80] Lam. 2:1.
[81] Lam. 1:6.
[82] Lam. 2:11.
[83] See Ovid, *Metamorphoses* 4.474, trans. by J. F. Miller (Loeb Classical Library; Cambridge, MA, 1916).
[84] Rev. 18:7.
[85] See Jer. 2:14.

wealthy and want for nothing. Little do you realize how wretched you are, how pitiable and poor, how blind and naked."[86]

Consider, O miserable one, how much darkness weighs on your soul; notice what thick, dark blindness engulfs you. Does the fury of lust impel you to the male sex? Has the madness of lust incited you to your own kind, that is, male to male? Does a [male] goat goaded by lust, ever sometimes leap on a [male] goat? Does a ram leap on a ram, maddened with the heat for sexual union? In fact a stallion feeds calmly and peacefully with a stallion in one stall and when he sees a mare the sense of lust is immediately unleashed. Never does a bull petulantly desire a bull out of love for sexual union; never does a mule bray under the stimulant for sex with a mule. But ruined men do not fear to commit what the very brutes shrink from in horror. What is committed by the rashness of human depravity is condemned by the judgment of irrational animals.

Unmanned man, speak! Respond, effeminate man! What do you seek in a male which you cannot find in yourself? What sexual difference? What different physical lineaments? What softness? What tender, carnal attraction? What pleasant, smooth face? Let the vigour of the male appearance terrify you, I beseech you; your mind should abhor virile strength. In fact, it is the rule of natural appetite that each seek beyond himself what he cannot find within the cloister of his own faculty. Therefore, if contact with male flesh delights you, turn your hand to yourself. Know that whatever you do not find in yourself, you seek vainly in another [male] body. Woe to you, unfortunate soul, at whose ruin angels are saddened and whom the enemy insults with applause. You are made the prey of demons, the rape of the cruel, the spoils of wicked men. "All your enemies open their mouths against you; they hiss and gnash their teeth. They say: We have devoured her; this at last is the day we hoped for; we found it, we saw it."[87]

[86] Rev. 3:17.
[87] Lam. 2:16.

XVIII

THE SOUL OUGHT TO BE MOURNED FOR BECAUSE IT DOES NOT MOURN

O miserable soul, I weep for you with so many lamentations because I do not see you weeping. I prostrate myself on the ground for you because I see you maliciously standing up after such a grave fall, even to the point of trying for the pinnacle of an ecclesiastical order. On the other hand, if you would bow down in humility, I, assured of your restoration, would exalt in the Lord with my whole body. If suitable compunction and contrition would strike the secret recesses of your heart, I, not improperly, would rejoice in a dance of unspeakable joy. This is the reason why you in particular should be wept for because you yourself are not weeping; this is why you need the commiseration of others—because you yourself are not saddened by the danger of your calamity. And you should be wept for with more bitter tears of fraternal compassion since you do not consider in dismay your own sad state.

Why do you pretend to consider the burden of your damnation? Now sunk into the depths of sins, now elevated to pride, why do you not cease "to store up retribution for yourself for that day of wrath?"[88] It is coming; the curse hurled from the mouth of David on Joab and on his house for the spilling of Abner's blood is coming upon you. The plague of Gomorrah now lives in the dwelling of your body—the pestilence which condemned the house of Joab with revenge for cruel homicide. In fact, when Abner was killed David said, "I and my

[88] Rom. 2:5.

kingdom are forever innocent of the blood of Abner, the son of Ner. And may it come upon the head of Joab, and upon all his father's house; and let there not fail from the house of Joab one doing a deed of Gomorrah."[89] For which a second translation reads, ". . . one suffering from a discharge of semen, or a leper, or one unmanly, one falling by the sword, or one in need of bread."[90]

In fact, a leper who is defiled with the stain of a grave sin is sprinkled; "to be unmanly" is to relinquish the strong deeds of a virile life and to exhibit the seductive weakness of feminine conversation. He "falls by the sword" who incurs the fury of divine wrath. He "needs bread" who is restrained by the punishment for his own guilt from the reception of the body of Christ who is the living bread come down from heaven.[91] Therefore, if after a flow of semen you become as a leper and are compelled to remain outside the camp by the precept of the Law,[92] why do you still try to obtain the primacy of honour in the same camp?

When King Uzziah proudly wished to burn incense on the altar of incense and after he knew he was struck from heaven with the blow of leprosy, he not only patiently bore being expelled from the temple by the priests, but did he not himself hasten to leave?[93] In fact, it is written, "Azariah the chief priest and all the other priests examined him, and saw the leprosy in his forehead; and they made haste to thrust him out," and it is added immediately, "And being frightened, he hastened to leave because he had felt the affliction of the Lord."[94]

If the king who was struck with bodily leprosy did not spurn being expelled from the temple by the priests, why do you, leprous soul, not accept being removed from the sacred altars on the basis of the judgment of so many holy fathers? If he was not ashamed to live in a private house until the end of his life, after giving up the rule of regal dignity, why are you disturbed about descending from the citadel of the sacerdotal office so that, enclosed in the sepulcher of penance, you might be eager to be numbered among the living as though you were dead?

---

[89] 2 Sam. 3:28-29. The expression "one doing a deed of Gomorrah" is not in the Vulgate.

[90] 2 Sam. 3:29. "One unmanly" translates the Latin "fusum tenens," which is literally, "one plying the spindle."

[91] See John 6:51.

[92] See Deut. 23:11-12.

[93] 2 Chron. 26:16-20.

[94] 2 Chron. 26:20.

To return to that mystical history of Joab: if you yourself have fallen by the sword, how will you raise another through priestly grace? If you, through lack of merits are in want of bread, that is, if you are separated from the body of Christ, how can you satisfy another with the heavenly feasts of the altar? If you are struck on the forehead with the leprosy of Uzziah, that is, if your face is dishonoured with the mark of infamy, how can you cleanse another from the flowing inundation of the crime that has been committed? So puffed up pride should blush with shame and not vainly desire to be extolled above itself—a pride not a little crushed by the burden of its own guilt. It should learn to ponder its own evils with subtle consideration; let it learn to live within the bounds of its own measure in humility lest, while it arrogantly usurps what it is powerless to obtain, true humility certainly loses what it could have hoped for.

XIX

THE SERVICE OF AN UNWORTHY PRIEST IS THE RUIN OF THE PEOPLE

O guilty, carnal men, why do you desire the height of ecclesiastical dignity with so much burning ambition? Why is it that you try with such desire to ensnare the people of God in the bonds of your own ruin? Is it not enough for you to throw yourselves down the steep cliffs of outrageous crime without having to involve others in the peril of your own ruin?

Suppose someone comes to ask us to intercede for him with a powerful man who is angry with him, and suppose we do not know this powerful man. We would immediately respond: We are unable to come to intercede because we are not familiar with him. So, if someone is bashful about interceding with a man of whom he presumes little, in what frame of mind does a person who does not know whether he is a friend of God's grace through the merits of his life occupy the place of intercession with God for the people? Or how can anyone who does not know whether he himself is pleasing to God ask God for forgiveness for others? In this something else must be more anxiously feared, namely, that the one who is believed to be able to placate anger merit it himself because of his own guilt. We all know clearly that when anyone who is displeasing is sent to intercede, the irritated soul is provoked to worse things.

Therefore, the person who is still bound by earthly desires should beware lest, by more gravely igniting the anger of the strict Judge, he become the author of the ruin of his subordinates while he takes pleasure in his exalted position. So, if culpable vice still rules over him, a person should prudently take stock of himself before he dares to assume the position of the sacerdotal office, lest one who is perverted by his own crime should desire to become the intercessor for the faults of others. Be careful, be careful, and be afraid of igniting inextinguishably God's fury towards you; fear lest you provoke more sharply by your very prayers the one you offend openly by acting evilly. Intent on your own ruin, beware of becoming responsible for the ruin of another. The more moderately you now fall into sin, the more easily will you rise by means of the outstretched hand of penance through the mercy of God.

XX

GOD REFUSES TO ACCEPT THE SACRIFICE
FROM THE HANDS OF THE UNCLEAN

And if almighty God himself disdains to receive the sacrifice from your hands, who are you to presume to throw yourself importunately on him who refuses? "In fact, the sacrifice of the wicked is an abomination to the Lord."[95] But you who are angry with me and who hate to listen to this writer, at least hear him who speaks to you with a prophetic voice; hear him, I say, preaching, thundering, rejecting your sacrifices, publicly crying out against your offerings. For Isaiah, the greatest of the prophets, says—indeed, the Holy Spirit through the mouth of Isaiah says:

> Hear the word of the Lord, princes of Sodom! Listen to the instruction of our God, people of Gomorrah! What care I for the number of your sacrifices? says the Lord. I have had enough of whole-burnt rams and fat of fatlings; in the blood of calves, lambs, and goats I find no pleasure. When you come in to visit me, who asks these things of you? Trample my courts no more! Bring no more worthless offerings; your incense is loathsome to me. New moon and sabbath, calling of assemblies, octaves with wickedness: these I cannot bear. Your new moons and festivals I detest; they weigh me down, I tire of the load. When you spread out your hands, I close my eyes to you; though you pray the more, I will not listen. Your hands are full of blood.[96]

[95] Prov. 15:8.
[96] Isa. 1:10-15.

So take note that although the judgment of divine correction bears on all evil vices together, nevertheless it is principally hurled down on the princes of the Sodomites and the people of Gomorrah. Consequently, if it perhaps shrinks from believing a human witness as to how mortal a vice this is, at least let the rashness of the complainers give in to divine testimony.

Perhaps someone will use as an objection against us that it is the divine intention[97] that the prophet's words, "Your hands are full of blood," are to be understood to refer to homicide and not to impurity of the flesh. However, such a one should realize that all sins are called blood in the divine writings. David is a witness to this when he says, "Free me from blood guilt, O God, my saving God."[98] Indeed, if we apply ourselves to examine the nature of this vice carefully and recall to memory the statements of the physicists,[99] we find that a flow of semen originates from blood. For just as the water of the sea is changed to foam by the agitation of the winds, so blood is excited to the humour of semen by the contracting of the genitals. Therefore, it is rightly believed to be consistent with a sound understanding if the statement, "your hands are full of blood," should seem to be said of the plague of impurity. And this was perhaps the case because the punishment against Joab arose from no other fault than from the shedding of blood so that the one who willingly shed another's blood was struck down with a just punishment if he was unwilling to bear the shedding of his own blood.

But since we have arrived, through a long disputation, at the point where we have clearly shown the Lord himself condemning and legally prohibiting the sacrifices of the impure, why are we sinners surprised if our admonition is rejected by them? If we see the command of the divine voice taken lightly by the puffed up heart of the reprobate, why is it surprising if we who are on earth are not believed?

[97] The Latin text reads "divinae inventionis" (PL 145, 181C).

[98] Ps. 51:16. See Peter Damian, Opusc. 34 (PL 145, 579B); Opusc. 56 (PL 145, 818A).

[99] See Isidore, *Etymologiarum sive originum libri XX*, ed. by W. M. Lindsay (Oxford, 1911), Book 6.4.

XXI

NO HOLY OFFERING WHICH IS SOILED WITH THE CRIMES OF IMPURITY IS RECEIVED BY GOD

For he who despises the councils of the holy fathers which should be revered, who rejects the precepts of the apostles and of apostolic men, who does not fear to set aside the edicts of canonical sanction, who takes lightly the command of divine authority itself, must be admonished at least to place before his eyes the day of his calling. He should not doubt that the severity of the judgment against him will be in proportion to the gravity of his sin. As the angel says in reference to Babylon, "In proportion to her boasting and sensuality, repay her in torment and grief!"[100] He must be warned to consider that as long as he continues to be afflicted by the sickness of this vice, even if he is seen to do something good, he still does not merit a reward. Nor is any act of religion, any mortification, any perfection of life which is defiled by such stains of foul impurity worthwhile before the eyes of the heavenly Judge.

However, the testimony of Venerable Bede will be adduced to prove that this is true. He says, "He who gives alms but does not abandon the fault does not redeem his soul, which he does not restrain from vices."[101] This is confirmed by the deeds of a hermit who served with many virtues in the company of a certain colleague. The following thought was suggested to the hermit by the devil: whenever he was

---

[100] Rev. 18:7.
[101] Unidentified in Bede.

76

aroused by lust, he should release semen by rubbing his genitals, just as he blows mucus from his nose. For this he was handed over to the demons at death while his friend was looking on. Then the same friend, not knowing his guilt but recalling his exercise of the virtues, almost despaired saying, "O, who can be saved? How has he perished?" An angel standing nearby said to him, "Don't be disturbed; for although he did many things, nonetheless he soiled everything through this vice which the Apostle calls impurity."

XXII

ALL FOUR OF THE MODES ENUMERATED ABOVE ARE AGAINST NATURE

No one should flatter himself that he does not fall together with another, if he fell by himself into the contamination of lustful attraction, since the unhappy hermit who was given over to the demons at the moment of death did not pollute anyone else but was instructed to ruin himself through impurity. For just as different shoots emerge from one clump of vine, so the four offshoots which we listed above arise from one sodomite impurity, as from a most poisoned root. Consequently, when a person plucks a plagued cluster of grapes from any of them he perishes instantly, infected indifferently with poison. "They are a branch of Sodom's vine-stock, and from the vineyards of Gomorrah. Poisonous are the grapes and bitter their clusters."[102]

The serpent which we tried to crush with the stake of our disputation is four-headed; it bites with the fangs of any one of its heads and immediately injects its whole evil poison. Therefore, whether one pollutes himself or another in any manner whatsoever, even if discretion is observed, nevertheless he is undoubtedly to be convicted of having committed the crime of Sodom. Nor do we read that the inhabitants of Sodom corrupted others only by the consummated act. We should rather believe that under the impulse of unbridled lust they acted shamefully alone and with others in different ways. Clearly, if any room for forgiveness were offered for the ruin caused by this vice, to whom would indulgent forgiveness be more readily fitting than to that

[102] Deut. 32:32.

hermit, for instance, who sinned without knowing—the hermit who fell through simple inexperience, who thought that this was permitted him as a right arising from a natural function?

Learn miserable ones, learn to restrain yourselves from the plague of such detestable vice, to tame manfully the lascivious pimping of lust, to repress the petulant incentive of the flesh, to fear to the marrow the terrible judgment of divine severity. Always recall the judgment of divine warning which says, "It is a fearful thing to fall into the hands of the living God."[103] Recall also the fearsome, menacing cry of the prophet when he says, "Because in the fire of the jealousy of the Lord the whole earth shall be consumed and all flesh on his sword."[104] For if carnal men are to be destroyed by the divine sword, why do they now culpably love this flesh? Indeed, this is the sword which the Lord directs against sinners through Moses, saying, "I will sharpen, as lightning, my sword."[105] And again, "My sword shall gorge itself with flesh."[106] That is: my fury will swallow up those living in the pleasure of the flesh. Just as those who fight against the monsters of vice are aided by the help of heavenly strength, so, on the contrary, those dedicated to the impurity of the flesh are given over to the sole judgment of divine vengeance. As Peter says, "The Lord knows how to rescue devout men from trial, and how to continue the punishment of the wicked up to the day of judgment. He knows, especially, how to treat those who live for the flesh in their desire for whatever corrupts."[107] And exclaiming elsewhere against these he says, "Thinking daytime revelry a delight, they are stain and defilement as they share your feasts in a spirit of seduction. They have eyes set on adultery and turned unceasingly towards sin."[108]

Nor should those who are placed in sacred orders boast if they live in a detestable way, since the higher they stand in eminence, the deeper they are cast down when they fall. Just as they ought now to precede others in a holy way of life, so afterwards they will be compelled to undergo more atrocious sufferings, since, according to the voice of Peter, "God did not spare the angels who sinned. He held them captive

[103] Heb. 10:31.
[104] Zeph. 1:18.
[105] Deut. 32:41.
[106] Deut. 32:42.
[107] 2 Pet. 2:9-10.
[108] 2 Pet. 2:13-14.

in Tartarus—consigned them to pits of darkness, to be guarded until judgment. And he condemned the cities of Sodom and Gomorrah to destruction, reducing them to ashes, making them an example to those who in the future should live impiously."[109]

Why is it that he immediately turns to the destruction of Sodom and Gomorrah after recounting the fall into diabolical damnation unless, as he clearly shows, because those who now are given over to the vice of impurity are to be damned together with the impure spirits in eternal punishment? Those who are now troubled by the ardour of sodomite lust afterwards will also burn along with the author of all iniquity in the flames of perpetual burning. The apostle Jude also agrees with this view, saying, "There were angels, too, who did not keep to their own domain, who deserted their dwelling place. These the Lord has kept in perpetual bondage, shrouded in murky darkness against the judgment of the great day. Sodom and Gomorrah, and the towns there about indulged in lust, just as those angels did; they practised unnatural vice. They are set before us to dissuade us as they undergo a punishment of eternal fire."[110] It is clear, therefore, that just as the angels who did not respect their pre-eminence merited the torment of the darkness of Tartarus, so those who fall from the dignity of sacred orders into the abyss of carnal vice are justly turned over to the pit of eternal damnation.

Let me conclude all of this: whoever has defiled himself with the contagion of abominable shamefulness in any of the ways we distinguished above, unless purged by the satisfaction of fruitful penance, can never have the grace of God, is never worthy of the body and blood of Christ, will never cross the threshold of the heavenly fatherland. The apostle John clearly declares this in the Apocalypse. When speaking of the glory of the heavenly kingdom he adds, "Nothing defiled shall enter it nor anyone who has done a detestable act."[111]

[109] 2 Pet. 2:4, 6.
[110] Jude 6-7.
[111] Rev. 21:27.

XXIII

AN EXHORTATION TO ARISE TO ONE FALLEN INTO SIN WITH MEN

Arise, I beg of you; rouse yourself, O man weighed down with the lethargy of miserable pleasure. Then come back to life, you who have fallen by the deadly sword before your enemies. The apostle Paul is present. Hear him crying out, shouting, admonishing, and crying at you with a clear voice, "Awake, O sleeper, from the dead, and Christ will revive you."[112] Why are you who hear the risen Christ diffident about your own resurrection? Hear from his own mouth, "Whoever believes in me, though he should die, will come to life."[113] If life-giving life seeks to raise you, why do you put up with falling farther towards your own death? Beware, beware, therefore, lest the pit of desperation swallow you up. Your mind should confidently presume on divine piety lest the impenitent harden because of the magnitude of his crime. So it is not for sinners to despair, but for the impious; nor does the magnitude of crimes lead the soul to desperation, although impiety does. For if the devil alone is able to drown you in the depths of this vice, how much more can the strength of Christ recall you to the height from which you fell? "He who has fallen, will he not do more to arise?"[114] The mule of your flesh has fallen into the mud under the weight; it is the goad of penance which fights; it is the hand of the Spirit which manfully pulls you out.

[112] Eph. 5:14.
[113] John 11:25.
[114] See Ps. 41:9 (Vulgate). However, the Vulgate reads "sleeps" for "fallen."

That most strong man Samson not only lost the seven hairs by which his strength was preserved because he wickedly opened the secret of his heart to a flattering woman, but being made the plunder of Allophylis, he lost his eyes. However, with hair restored, he afterwards humbly sought the aid of the Lord his God, straddled the temple of Dagon, and destroyed a much greater multitude of the enemy than before.[115] Therefore, if your soft, impure flesh deceptively persuaded you, if it banished the seven gifts of the Holy Spirit, if it extinguished not the light of the brow but of the heart, you should not be dispirited, do not completely despair, but collect your strength, act manfully, presume to try brave things. In this way you will be able to triumph over your enemies by the mercy of God. Certainly, the Philistines were indeed able to shave Samson's hair, but not to pluck it out. So, although the evil spirits might deprive you of the charism of the Holy Spirit for a time, nonetheless, they can never prevail by denying the remedy of divine reconciliation without chance of recovery. How, I ask, can you despair of the most bountiful mercy of the Lord who even blamed the Pharaoh for not flying to the remedy of penance after sin? Hear what he says, "I have broken the arms of Pharaoh, the king of Egypt, and have not been asked to give him health and that strength be returned to him to hold the sword."[116]

What will I say of Ahab, king of Israel? After he fashioned idols, after impiously killing Naboth the Jezreelite, nonetheless, just as on the one hand he humbled himself, so on the other hand he received mercy. Scripture attests that after he was frightened by the divine warning, "he tore his garments and put on sackcloth over his flesh. He fasted, slept in the sackcloth, and walked about with his head cast down."[117] And what after this? "Then the Lord said to Elijah the Tishbite: Have you seen that Ahab has humbled himself before me? Since he has humbled himself before me I will not bring the evil in his time."[118] Consequently, if the penance of the one who did not know how to persevere is not despised, why are you diffident about the largess of divine mercy if you try unstintingly to persevere? Establish an unremitting contest against the flesh; with weapons always ready, stand against the importunate madness of lust. If the flame of lust

[115] See Judg. 16.
[116] See Ezek. 30:21. Damian's text differs considerably from the Vulgate.
[117] 1 Kings 21:27.
[118] 1 Kings 21:28-29.

burns to the bones, the memory of perpetual fire should extinguish it immediately. If the cunning attacker presents the smooth face of the flesh, the mind should immediately direct the eyes to the sepulchers of the dead and attend wisely to whether what is found there is soft to the touch and pleasing to the eye.[119]

He should consider that the slime which now rots unbearably, that the bloody matter which breeds and feeds worms, that whatever dust, whatever dry ashes are seen thrown there, were once beautiful flesh which was subject to such passions in its prime. Finally, consider the rigid sinews, the bare teeth, the torn compact of bones and joints, the terribly rotted composition of all the members. In this way he extracts the monstrous vision of unformed and confused imagination from the human heart. Consider, then, what a dangerous transformation follows because of the fleeting pleasure caused by the momentary emission of semen—a transformation which does not end throughout the course of thousands of years. Think how miserable it is that because of the present satisfaction of one organ's pleasure, afterwards the whole body together with the soul will be tortured forever by the most atrocious, flaming fires. By these and similar impenetrable mental shields ward off imminent evils, and wipe out the past by penance. Fasting breaks the pride of the flesh; the mind grows fat with the feasts of assiduous prayer. In this way the protector of the spirit coerces the flesh into subjection by means of the bridle of discipline,[120] and daily strives to hasten to the heavenly Jerusalem on the fervent steps of longing.

[119] See P. Damian, Opusc. 15.23, "The recollection of death and burial is very beneficial against all temptations" (PL 145, 355A-56A).

[120] While the term "discipline" undoubtedly refers to a general control over the flesh, it may also refer here to flagellation, frequently recommended by Damian. See Opusc. 43, "De laudo flagellorum et, ut loquuntur, disciplinae" (PL 145, 679A-86C), and J. Leclercq, *Saint Pierre Damien*, 100-105.

XXIV

TO CONQUER LUST IT IS ENOUGH TO CONTEMPLATE THE REWARDS OF CHASTITY

The reward of this labour is that you continually look on the promised rewards of chastity, and whatever cunning the sly instigator opposes, you will overcome by the unshackled feet of faith. If happiness is attended to, which is not attained without a transition, the labour of transition becomes light. The hired labourer eases the tedium of his work when he eagerly anticipates the wages which are due his work. Therefore, weigh what is said through the prophet about the soldiers of chastity, "Thus says the Lord: To the eunuchs who observe my sabbaths and choose what pleases me and hold fast to my covenant, I will give, in my house and within my walls, a monument and a name better than sons and daughters."[121]

In fact, those who repress the immoderate impetus of the flesh are eunuchs, and they cut away from themselves the effect of the evil work. However, many of those who serve the pleasures of carnal enticement desire to leave the memory of their name behind them through succeeding generations of offspring. They desire this with the whole affection of their minds because they believe that they will never completely die to this world if they perpetuate the title of their name through the offshoot of their surviving offspring.

However, celibates more clearly and with happier results accept this duty to which the common people are inflamed with the ardour of such

[121] Isa. 56:4-5.

fiery ambition, since the memory of celibates lives on forever with him who does not pass through the state of eternity according to the law of time. Therefore, the divine voice promises a name to eunuchs which is better than sons and daughters, since the memory of a name which future generations of sons could extend throughout a brief space of time, these merit to possess forever without the detriment of oblivion. "The just man shall be in everlasting remembrance."[122] And again it is said through John in the Apocalypse, "They shall walk with me in white because they are worthy, and I will not erase their names from the book of life."[123] Again it is said in the same place, "These are men who were not defiled with women, for they are virgins and follow the Lamb wherever he goes."[124] They sing the canticle which no one can sing except that hundred and forty-four thousand.[125] In fact it is an exclusive canticle which the virgins sing to the Lamb, because they rejoice with him forever over the incorruption of the flesh ahead of all the faithful. Clearly the rest of the just cannot pronounce it although they merit to hear it since they are placed in the same beatitude. Indeed, they rejoice in the splendour of virgins without, however, gaining their rewards. Accordingly, we must give thought to and very carefully consider the highest state where such great excellence and the ultimate in happiness are to be found, where it is most blessed to preserve the paternal laws of equity. As Truth attests, "Not everyone accepts this teaching"[126] in this world, so not all reach that glory of the supreme reward in the future.

Dear brother whoever you are, consider these and other such [testimonies] within the recesses of your mind, and with all your strength rush to keep your flesh immune from every lustful plague so that, in accord with the judgment of apostolic teaching, "you might know how to guard your member in sanctity and honour, not in passionate desire as do the Gentiles who know not God."[127] If you are standing up to now, beware of a fall;[128] if you fall, confidently turn your hand to the scalpel of penance which is readily available. If you were unable to

[122] Ps. 112:6.
[123] Rev. 3:4-5.
[124] Rev. 14:4.
[125] Rev. 14:3.
[126] Matt. 19:11.
[127] 1 Thes. 4:4-5.
[128] See 1 Cor. 10:12.

spend time with Abraham far from the Sodomites, it is permitted to migrate with Lot, urged on by the destructive burning which is near at hand.[129] If you cannot approach the port unharmed in a ship, it is enough at least to have avoided the shipwreck of the swamping waves. And those of you who have not deserved to reach the safety of shore without loss, seeing the sand after the danger, should be free to sing with the rhythmic voice of blessed Jonah, "All your breakers and your billows passed over me. Then I said: I was banished from your sight! Yet would I again look upon your holy temple."[130]

[129] See Gen. 18:16-19, 29.
[130] Jon. 2:4-5.

XXV

THE WRITER CREDIBLY EXCUSES
HIMSELF

Now, this little book might fall into the hands of someone whose conscience completely disapproves of it and who may be displeased, perhaps, by what is included above and accuse me of being a traitor and an informer on the crime of a brother. He should know that I eagerly focus my whole intention on seeking the favour of the internal Judge, and that in truth I do not fear the hatred of the depraved or the tongues of detractors. In fact, I would rather be cast innocent into the cistern with Joseph, who accused his brothers to his father for a terrible crime,[131] than to be punished by the vengeance of divine fury with Eli, who saw the evils of his sons and was silent.[132] For when the divine voice issues a terrible threat through the mouth of the prophet and says, "If you see your brother doing evil and you do not correct him I will require his blood from your hand,"[133] who am I to see such a harmful outrage growing up among the sacred orders and, as a murderer of another's soul, preserve the stricture of silence,[134] and to dare to await the reckoning of divine severity? Do I not begin to be

---

[131] See Gen. 37.

[132] See 1 Sam. 2. Damian frequently uses the account of Eli against ecclesiastical superiors who do not correct the sexual abuses of their subordinates; see Opusc. 17.2 (PL 145, 383A-84B).

[133] See Ezek. 3:20.

[134] The expression "censura silentii" is used several times by Damian and seems best translated "stricture of silence." See Opusc. 13 (PL 145, 318C); Opusc. 14 (PL 145, 332D); Opusc. 47 (PL 145, 713B); Letter 1.13 (PL 144, 219D).

responsible for a guilt whose author I never was? And while Scripture says, "Cursed he who holds back his sword from blood,"[135] you urge me, with the sword of my tongue put up in the sheath of silence, to destroy myself while it contracts the rust of discredit. It is no help to others if it does not strike the faults of those who live wickedly. In fact, to hold back the sword from blood is to hold in check the word of correction from striking a carnal life. It is said again of this sword, "A sharp, two-edged sword came out of his mouth."[136]

How do I love my neighbour as myself if, through negligence, I allow to spread in his heart the wound from which, I have no doubt, he dies cruelly? Therefore, when I see minds being wounded will I neglect to cure with the surgery of words? The great preacher does not instruct me to do this. He believed himself innocent of the blood of his neighbours insofar as he did not hold back from attacking their vices. He says, "Therefore, I solemnly declare this day that I am innocent of the blood of all; for I have not shrunk from announcing to you God's design in its entirety."[137] John has not instructed me in this fashion when he provides me with the angelic admonition, "Say to him who hears: come."[138] Clearly, then, it is the task of one to whom an internal voice speaks to serve notice to others about the message he has been given, even to shout this message; otherwise, having remained silent, he might find the doors closed to him when he approaches them.

Indeed, if you think it valid to attack me who am on the attack and, as I might say, to accuse me of presumptuous prattle, why do you not reprove Jerome who disputed so sharply against different sects of heretics? Why not lash out against Ambrose who publicly harangued the Arians? Why not lash out against Augustine who, as a most austere disputant, inveighed against the Manichees and Donatists.[139] You say to me, "It is all right for them since they opposed heretics and blasphemers; however, you are not afraid of picking on Christians." To this I reply briefly: just as they strove to bring the erring and those who were leaving back to the fold, so it is also our intention to prevent in whatever way possible those who are inside from leaving. They said,

---

[135] Jer. 48:10.
[136] Rev. 1:16.
[137] Acts 20:26-27.
[138] Rev. 22:17.
[139] Reference to three outstanding Fathers of the Latin church: Jerome (ca. 342-420), Ambrose (ca. 339-97), Augustine (354-430).

"It was from our ranks that they took their leave—not that they really belonged to us; for if they had belonged to us, they would have stayed with us."[140] And we say: Indeed they are with us, but in a wicked way. Therefore, let us strive, if possible, that they be with us finally in a good way.

And we add this: if blasphemy is the worst, I do not know in what way sodomy is better. Blasphemy makes a man to err; sodomy, to perish. The former divides the soul from God; the latter joins it to the devil. The former casts out of paradise; the latter drowns in Tartarus. The former blinds the eyes of the mind; the latter casts into the turmoil of ruin. If we are careful to search into which of these crimes weighs more heavily on the scales of divine scrutiny, sacred scripture fully instructs us in what we seek. Indeed, while the sons of Israel were led into captivity for blaspheming God and worshipping idols, the Sodomites perished in heavenly fire and sulphur, devoured in the holocaust.

I have not proposed the holy doctors to presume to compare a smoky firebrand to the stars as if it were brighter. In fact, I recall such superlatively excellent men with an unworthy voice and scarcely without offence; but I say this since they taught younger men how they should act by what they did in correcting and confounding vices. Though in their time this plague had sprung up with such shameless freedom, we confidently believe that large volumes excerpted from the codices would seem [to be necessary] against it today. Therefore, no one should censure me when I dispute against mortal vice inasmuch as I am not trying to reproach but rather to promote fraternal salvation, lest while he persecute the reprover he might seem to favour the delinquent.

To use the words of Moses, "Whoever is for the Lord, let him come to me."[141] That is: whoever sees himself as a soldier of Christ should fervently gird himself to confound this vice, and not hesitate to wipe it out with all his strength. He should pierce it with the sharpest verbal arrows wherever it is found and try to slay it since, while the captor is surrounded by a great deployment of troops, the captive is freed from those bonds by which he is held in slavery. While the harmonious voice of everyone cries in unison against the tyrant, he who was dragged

[140] 1 John 2:19.
[141] Exod. 32:26.

away blushes at once to become the prey of the mad monster. And he who does not doubt, because of the acclaimed testimony of many, that he is snatched off to death, when he takes stock of himself is not slow to return to life as soon as possible.

XXVI

THE WORK IS DIRECTED TO THE LORD POPE

And now at the end of this work we return to you, most blessed Pope. We recall to you the point of this composition so that just as it was directed to you at the beginning so the closing of the completed work may fittingly end with you. Consequently, we ask and humbly impore Your Clemency, if it is legitimate to speak, that you prudently inspect the decrees of the sacred canons which, nevertheless, are well known to you. You should approve spiritual and prudent men to consult about this necessary investigation, and you should reply to us regarding these chapters so as to remove all scrupulous doubt from our breast. Nor do we presume to say this as if we did now know that with God's help your profound expertise alone is enough; but as long as the testimony of sacred authority is used and the matter is dealt with through the judgment and consensus of many, the complaint of perverse men, which perhaps would not be ashamed to murmur in dissent, may be quieted. For a complaint set against the judgment of many is not easily sustained. Moreover, a statement brought forward by one person in terms of the consideration of the law of equity is rejected by others as prejudice.

Therefore, with the four different kinds of this vice which we enumerated above carefully investigated, it would be gracious of your beatitude mercifully to instruct me with a decretal writing as to which of those guilty of these vices ought to be deposed irrevocably from ecclesiastical orders; and to whom, truly taking the view of discretion, this office can be mercifully granted; whether one who has fallen in any of the above mentioned ways, and with how many, should be allowed to remain in ecclesiastical dignity; how and with how many would he have to be defiled to be compelled to cease in the above mentioned necessity? Let many persons, labouring under the same ignorance, be instructed by what is directed to one person, seeing that the light of your authority removes the darkness of our doubt. And, as I might say, may the plough of the Apostolic See tear up by the roots the seed of all error from the field of a wavering conscience.

Most revered father, may almighty God grant that the monster of this vice completely perish during the time of your apostolate, and the state of the sick Church arise to its rightful vigour.

APPENDIX

LETTER OF POPE LEO IX TO PETER DAMIAN

The following translation of the letter of Pope Leo IX, "Ad splendidum nitentis," in reply to Peter Damian's Book of Gomorrah, *is reprinted from J. Boswell,* Christianity, Social Tolerance, and Homosexuality, *365-66, with kind permission of the University of Chicago Press.*

The final part of the last sentence of the third last paragraph in Boswell reads, "or—what is horrible to mention as well as to hear—who have fallen into the last category." The modification I have introduced is probably closer to the meaning. Boswell's note to this sentence: "Or, 'who have moved on to the rear'—a more literal reading of the words 'in terga praelapsi sunt'—but this seems inconsistent with the euphemistic terminology which otherwise characterizes the epistle" (p. 366).

Boswell's note concluding the translation: "See pp. 211-12 above. Text in Mansi, 19:685-86. The ponderous complexity of the Latin text, characteristic of official letters, is reflected in the somewhat awkward translation" (p. 366).

Bishop Leo, servant of the servants of God, to the hermit Peter beloved son in Christ, the joy of eternal beatitude. [Omitted by Boswell.]

The book which you have published, my son, against the fourfold pollution of carnal contagion, frank in style and even more direct in reasoning, provides indisputable evidence of the intention of your mind to enter the holy fray on the side of the splendid might of shining modesty. You have indeed smitten wantonness of the flesh by thus striking with the arm of the spirit against obscene desire, clearly delineating the execrable vice by the authority of virtue, which, since it is itself immaculate, allows no uncleanness. Nor could it ever be the sort of thing which would lend itself to sordid vanities. Indeed these clerics concerning whose disgusting lives your wisdom has discoursed mournfully, fairly, and reasonably are rightly—altogether rightly— excluded from [literally, "do not belong to"] the bond of its inheritance, from which they have cut themselves off with voluptuous pleasures. Because if they lived chastely, they might be called not only the holy temple of God but also the sanctuary, in which the Lamb of God is sacrificed in shining glory, through whom the horrid filth of the whole world is cleansed. Such clerics, of course, reveal by the testimony of their deeds, if not their words, that they are not what they are thought to be. For how could anyone be or even be called a cleric when he has not feared to do evil through his own will?

About these things, since you have written what seemed best to you, moved by holy indignation, it is appropriate that as you wish, we interpose our apostolic authority, so that we may remove any scrupulous doubt among those reading [this], and that it may be clear to all that the things contained in this little book, like water thrown on the fires of hell, have met with our approval. Therefore, lest the unpunished license of filthy desire should spread, it is essential to combat [it] with appropriate measures of apostolic severity, and moreover to give some evidence of strictness.

Even though all those polluted by the filth of any of the four types [of this sin] mentioned are excluded from all rank in the spotless church by the just censure of equity—both that of sacred councils and by our own judgment—yet we, acting more humanely, desire and ordain that those who elicited their seed either with their own hands or mutually with someone else, and even those who spilled it interfemorally, if it was not a long-standing practice or performed with many men and if they have restrained their desires and atoned for these shameful sins with a suitable penance, should be admitted to the same rank which they held while in sin (though they must no longer remain so), trusting in divine mercy. But there may be no hope of recovering their rank for those who are tainted with either of the two types of sin you have described—alone or with others—for a long time or with many men even for a short time, or—what is horrible to mention as well as to hear—who have fallen into anal relations.

If anyone shall dare to criticize or question this decree of apostolic direction, let him know that he is himself acting in peril of his rank. For he who does not attack vice encourages it; such a one is rightly accounted guilty [and worthy] of the [same] end as he who perishes through sin.

But, beloved son, I rejoice inexpressibly that you demonstrate with the example of your life just what you have taught with the gift of your words. For it is greater to instruct by deed than by word. Wherefore, God willing, you shall earn the branch of victory and rejoice with the Son of God and the Virgin in the abode of heaven, and for every one of that crowd saved by you from the fires of the devil you shall be crowned and rewarded with graces.

BIBLIOGRAPHY

1. Ancient and Medieval

Abelard, Peter. *Sic et Non*. Translation of "Prologue" in B. Polka and B. Zelechow, *Readings in Western Civilization*. Vol. 1, *The Intellectual Adventure of Man to 1600*, 102-14. Toronto, 1970.

Albers, B. "Wann sind die Beda-Egbert'schen Bussbücher verfasst worden, und wer ist ihr Verfasser?" *Archiv für katholisches Kirchenrecht* 81 (1901), 393-420.

Ansegisus. *Ansegisi abbatis capitularium collectio*. In A. Boretius, *Capitularia regum francorum*, Vol. 1, 382ff.; and PL 97, 503-84.

Anselm. *Historia dedicationis ecclesiae s. Remigii apud Remos*. PL 142, 1415-40.

Benedictus Levita. *Capitularia*. PL 97, 699-912.

Bieler, L. *The Irish Penitentials*. With an appendix by D. A. Binchy. Scriptores Latini Hiberniae, 5. Dublin, 1963.

Bonizo of Sutri. *Bonizo: Liber de vita christiana*. Edited by E. Perels. Berlin, 1930.

Burchard of Worms. *Decretum*. PL 140, 537-1058.

Caesar. *The Gallic War*. Translated by H. J. Edwards. The Loeb Classical Library. Cambridge, MA, 1917.

Collectio Dionysio-Hadriana. PL 67, 139-346.

Collectio Hispana. PL 84, 93-848.

Collection in Two Books. J Bernhard, "La Collection en deux livres (Cod. Vat. lat. 3822)." *Revue de droit canonique* 12 (1962).

Collection in 74 Titles. J. T. Gilchrist, *Diversorum patrum sentente sive Collectio in LXXIV titulos digesta*. Monumenta iuris canonici. Series B.: Corpus collectionum, 1. Vatican, 1973.

Damian, Peter. *S. Petri Damiani opera omnia*. Edited by C. Gaetani. PL 144-45.

——————. *Liber gratissimus*. Edited by L. Von Heinemann. MGH, Libelli de lite 1, 15-75.

Fructuosus. C. W. Barlow, *Rule for the Monastery of Compludo*. The Fathers of the Church, 63. Washington, DC, 1969.

Gregory I. *Registrum epistolarum*. MGH, Epistolae, vol. 2. Edited by L. M. Hartmann. Berlin, 1899.

Herard of Tours. *Capitula*. PL 121, 763-74.

Hincmar of Reims. *Capitula*. PL 125, 777-92.

Isidore of Seville. *Etymologiarum sive originum libri XX*. Edited by W. M. Lindsay. Oxford, 1911.

Jerome. *Commentariorum in Matheum libri IV*. Edited by D. Hurst and M.Adriaen. Corpus christianorum series latina, 7. Turnhout, 1969.

_____ . *Liber de nominibus Hebraicis*. PL 23, 815-904.

John Chrysostom. *Jean Chrysostome à Theodore*. Translated and edited by J. Dumortier. Sources chrétiennes, 117. Paris, 1966. English translation: W. R. Stephens, *An Exhortation to Theodore after his Fall*. Nicene and Post-Nicene Fathers. First Series, 9. New York, 1889.

John the Deacon. *Vita S. Gregorii Magni*. PL 75, 59-242.

Mansi, J. D. *Sacrorum conciliorum nova et amplissima collectio*. 31 vols. Florence and Venice, 1759-98.

Martianus Capella. *De nuptiis philologiae et Mercurii libri VIIII*. Edited by A. Dick, revised by J. Preaux. Stuttgart, 1969. English translation: *Martianus Capella and the Seven Liberal Arts*. Vol. 2, *The Marriage of Philology and Mercury*. Translated by W. H. Stahl and R. Johnson with E. L. Burge. Records of Civilization: Sources and Studies, 84. New York, 1977.

Ovid. *Metamorphoses*. Translated by J. F. Miller. The Loeb Classical Library. Cambridge, MA, 1916.

Rabanus Maurus. *Paenitentiale ad Otgarium*. PL 112, 1397-1424.

_____ . *Paenitentiale ad Heribaldum*. PL 110, 467-94.

Regino of Prüm. *Reginonis abbatis Prumiensis, libri duo de synodalibus causis et disciplinis ecclesiasticis*. Edited by H. Wasserschleben. Leipzig, 1840.

Rodulph of Bourges. *Capitula*. PL 119, 703-26.

Schmitz, H. J. *Dis Bussbücher und die Bussdisciplin der Kirche nach handschriftlichen Quellen dargestellt*. Mainz, 1883.

_____ . *Die Bussbücher und das kanonische Bussverfahren nach handschriftlichen Quellen dargestellt*. Düsseldorf, 1898.

Werminghoff, A. *Concilia aevi karolini*, vol. 1. MGH, Legum sectio 3, vol. 2. Hanover, 1906.

2. Studies

Bailey, D. S. *Homosexuality and the Western Christian Tradition*. London, 1955.

Blum, O. J. *St. Peter Damian: His Teaching on the Spiritual Life*. Washington, 1947.

_____ . "The Monitor of the Popes: St Peter Damian." *Studi Gregoriani* 2 (1947), 459-76.

Boswell, J. *Christianity, Social Tolerance, and Homosexuality: Gay People in Western Europe from the Beginning of the Christian Era to the Fourteenth Century*. Chicago, 1980.

Bullough, V. *Sexual Variance in Society and History*. A Wiley Interscience Publication. New York, 1976.

Canadian Churchman. 102/10 (1976).

Catholic Council for Church and Society (The Netherlands). *Homosexual People in Society*. Translated by B. A. Nachbahr. New Ways Ministry, 1980.

Cowdrey, H. E. J. *The Cluniacs and the Gregorian Reform*. Oxford, 1970.

De Clercq, C. *La législation religieuse franque de Clovis à Charlemagne: Etude sur les actes de conciles et les capitulaires, les statuts diocésains et les règles monastiques (507-814)*. Louvain, 1936.

Dressler, F. *Petrus Damiani: Leben und Werke*. Studia Anselmiana, vol. 34. Rome, 1954.

Finsterwalder, P. "Zwei Bischofskapitularien der Karolingerzeit." *Zeitschrift der Savigny-Stiftung für Rechtsgeschichte, kanonistische Abteilung* 14 (1925), 336-83.

Fliche, A. *La réforme grégorienne*. Vol. 1, *La formation des idées grégoriennes*. Paris, 1924.

Fournier, P. and G. Le Bras. *Histoire des collections canoniques en occident depuis les Fausses Décrétales jusqu'au Décret de Gratien*. 2 vols. Paris, 1931-32.

Gaudemet, J. "Les statuts épiscopaux de la première décade du IXe siècle." *Proceedings of the Fourth International Congress of Medieval Canon Law*. Edited by S. Kuttner. Monumenta Iuris canonici. Series C: Subsidia 5, 303-49. Vatican, 1976.

Gauthier, A. "La sodomie dans le droit canonique médiéval." In B. Roy (ed.), *L'érotisme au moyen âge: études présentées au troisième colloque de l'Institut d'études médiévales*. Montreal, 1977.

Giet, S. "Le concile de Reims de 1049." *Mémoires de la société d'agriculture, commerce, sciences et arts du département de la Marne* 75 (1960), 31-36.

Goodich, M. *The Unmentionable Vice: Homosexuality in the Later Medieval Period*. Santa Barbara, CA, 1979.

Hefele, K. J. *A History of the Christian Councils from the Original Documents to the Close of the Council of Nicaea, A.D. 325*. Translated by W. R. Clark. Edinburgh, 1894.

Hefele, K. J. and H. Leclercq. *Histoire des conciles*. 8 vols. Paris, 1907-21.

Human Sexuality: New Directions in American Catholic Thought. New York, 1977.

Kottje, R. *Die Bussbücher Halitgars von Cambrai und des Hrabanus Maurus: Ihre Überlieferung und ihre Quellen*. Beiträge zur Geschichte und Quellen des Mittelalters, 8. Berlin/New York, 1980.

Kuhn, L. *Petrus Damiani und seine Anschauungen über Staat und Kirche*. Karlsruhe, 1913.

Leclercq, J. *Saint Pierre Damien ermite et homme d'église*. Uomini et dottrine, 8. Rome, 1960.

_____ , F. Vandenbroucke, L. Bouyer. *The Spirituality of the Middle Ages*. Translated by the Benedictines of Holme Eden Abbey. New York, 1968.

Little, K. "The Personal Development of Peter Damian." In *Order and Innovation: Essays in Honor of Joseph R. Strayer*. Princeton, 1976. 317-41.

Lucchesi, G. "Clavis S. Petri Damiani." In *Studi su S. Pier Damiano . . .* , 1-215.

_____ . "Per una vita di san Pier Damiani. Componenti cronologiche et topografiche." In *San Pier Damiani*, vol. 1, 13-179; vol. 2, 13-160.

McNeill, J. J. *The Church and the Homosexual*. Kansas City, 1976.

McNeill, J. T., and H. M. Gamer. *Medieval Handbooks of Penance: A Translation of the Prinicpal* Libri poenitentiales *and Selections from Related Documents*. Records of Civilization: Sources and Studies, 29. New York, 1938.

Mazzotti, C. "Il celibato e la castità del clero in S. Pier Damiani," In *Studi su S. Pier Damiano . . .* , 343-56.

Mirbt, C. *Die Publizistik im Zeitalter Gregors VII*. Leipzig, 1894.

Reindel, K. "Studien zur Überlieferung der Werke des Petrus Damiani." *Deutsches Archiv* 15 (1959), 23-102; 16 (1960), 73-154; 18 (1962), 317-417.

Ryan, J. J. *Saint Peter Damiani and his Canonical Sources: A Preliminary Study in the Antecedents of the Gregorian Reform*. Toronto, 1956.

San Peir Damiano nel IX centenario della morte (1072-1972). Centro studi di richerche sulla antica provincia ecclesiastica Ravennate, 3 vols. Cesena, 1972, 1973.

Shotwell, J. T. and L. R. Loomis. *The See of Peter*. Records of Civilization: Sources and Studies. New York, 1927.

Studi su S. Pier Damiano in onore del Cardinale Amleto Giovanni Cicognani. Biblioteca Cardinale Gaetano Cicognani, 5. 2nd. edition. Faenza, 1970.

Ullman, W. *A Short History of the Papacy in the Middle Ages*. London: University Paperback, 1974.

Vogel, C. *Les "Libri Paenitentiales."* Typologie des sources du moyen âge occidental, 27. Turnhout, 1978.

Watkins, O.D. *A History of Penance. Being a Study of the Authorities*. 2 vols. London, 1920.

Weinberg, M. and A. Bell. *Homosexuality: An Annotated Bibliography*. New York, 1972.

Whitney, J. P. "Peter Damiani and Humbert." *The Cambridge Historical Journal* 1 (1925), 225-48.

_____ . *Hildebrandine Essays*. Cambridge, 1932.

BIBLICAL REFERENCES